"It's easy to write songs. It's hard to write good songs, where something uniquely 'you' comes up from the deep and makes its mark."

Eliza Gilkyson, p. 65

Contents

SUBSCRIBE TO *NO DEPRESSION* IN PRINT
STORE.NODEPRESSION.COM

ON THE COVER

Anyone can write a song, but writing a good song is a challenge. And songwriting is a bit of a mysterious art form. It's a different experience for every writer, and inspiration can come from the most unexpected places. To honor the craft of songwriting, we hired Philadelphia-based painter, illustrator, and consummate singer-songwriter fan Jessica Husband to envision the ideal writer's desk. She came back at us with a boundless landscape of color and magic, a river pouring through a guitar.

NO DEPRESSION TEAM
Chris Wadsworth *Publisher*
Kim Ruehl *Editor-in-Chief*
Stacy Chandler *Assistant Editor*
Brittney McKenna *News & Social Media Editor*
Isa Burke *Editorial Assistant*
Sonja Nelson *Advertising*
Henry Carrigan *Print Partnerships*
Maureen Cross *Finance/Operations*

WEB nodepression.com
TWITTER & INSTAGRAM @nodepression
FACEBOOK facebook.com/nodepressionmag

GENERAL INQUIRIES
info@nodepression.com

ONLINE ADVERTISING
advertising@nodepression.com

SUBSCRIPTIONS
store.nodepression.com

JOURNAL DESIGN & PRODUCTION
Marcus Amaker
Printed in Nashville, Tennessee, by Lithographics Inc.

No Depression is part of the FreshGrass Foundation.
freshgrass.org
ISBN-13: 978-0-9973317-8-3
©2017, FreshGrass, LLC

Inside covers: Lyrics from Townes Van Zandt's "Pancho & Lefty." Illustrations by Drew Christie.

Hello Stranger

BY KIM RUEHL

When I was 19, I met a man in Buffalo, New York, named Michael Meldrum. An incredibly talented guitarist and great lover of music, Michael's biggest affection was for the well-written song. Many songwriters who passed through Buffalo's tight-knit music community during  Michael's life will remember him as a sort of teacher, though I'm not sure if he ever actually provided formal music lessons to anyone. In my experiences with Michael, he never sat me down and said, "This is a good chord progression." But, over beers or coffee, he would get to ruminating on what makes a song a good song. He would talk about the responsibility a songwriter has — the opportunity — to give something meaningful to a roomful of strangers that they can't get anywhere else from anybody else. Sure, he would say, you can give them a catchy chorus of "Oh baby, baby," but you could also give them "Imagine" or "Somewhere Over the Rainbow."

The latter will always remind me of Michael. He was proud of the fact that it had been written by a Buffalonian, and he would occasionally perform it on his Takamine acoustic during a Nietzsche's open mic night, sandwiched between songs by Townes Van Zandt and some other, more obscure writer he'd happened upon.

I absorbed Michael's perspective on songwriting for the two years I spent living in Buffalo, before I moved out to Portland, Oregon, and set off on the rest of my life. But I have never forgotten the lesson he taught me about getting into the heart of a song. Anyone can come up with a catchy melody, and anyone can be honest through poetry. But it takes a combination of vision and persistence to land upon the truth.

Of course, every songwriter has their own process, but back when I was pursuing songwriting as a career, I always liked to sit on the edge of my bed to write a song. A melody would surface in my mind, and I'd sit down with my guitar to pluck out a bassline. That would lead me to a chord progression, which I'd strum until I found the right fingerpicking pattern. Then I would hum the melody against that, over and over, for hours if necessary, until words emerged. It was like peeling leaves off an artichoke, one after another, until all that remained was the heart. I sang it over and over again — on the couch, in my bed, in the bathroom, in the car, in front of a mirror, in my office, until I could make it through the song without crying. That's how I knew it was done. By then, it was muscle memory, and I could put it aside and move on to the next one.

I wrote hundreds of songs this way, which is not an exaggeration. I counted for a while, but lost count after 200, sometime in my early 20s. For this reason, I've never been impressed by critics or labels or artists who talk about a songwriter's prolificacy. Writing a lot of songs is not particularly challenging, just as taking a lot of photographs is not. Quantity does not make an artist's work art, and certainly not every song written by someone who has chosen art as their path could be called art either. Art is the objective; it's not always the result. That's why songwriters like me find other things to do for a living, while songwriters like Anaïs Mitchell, Ani DiFranco, and Jason Isbell — arguably a few of the best songwriters of my generation — have songwriting careers.

When I was living in New York City, doing the starving artist thing, I heard a veteran musician tell someone else that songwriting is not a smart path. If you can imagine yourself doing anything else with your life, he told them, then that's what you should be doing. Only stay in songwriting if you can't think of anything else you could do. It was those words that I thought of when I eventually put my songwriting aside to work in this field, writing about other people's songwriting and bringing the stories of songwriters out into the world. And, since I was hired by *No Depression* in 2008, those are the words that have driven me to continue my pursuit of music criticism, as I couldn't imagine doing anything at all else with my time. Until, that is, there *was* something else I could imagine doing.

And now, I have a book to write and another road to travel.

So it's somewhat cathartic that I end my run with *No Depression* by making this singer-songwriter issue. After all, I began my songwriting career in 1995, the same year *No Depression* launched its magazine career. Our lives have operated in parallel ever since, me and this little magazine. That I somehow magically wound up being instrumental in bringing it back to the page, after being hired to create a life for it out of print, is a somewhat ironic blessing for which I am grateful.

I'm grateful for so many things that have occurred in the past decade, including the legacy of intelligent, inquisitive music journalism that I inherited from founding editors Peter Blackstock and Grant Alden. I look forward to reading where ND's next editor-in-chief take that legacy. I'll keep reading if you will.

Songs We Wish We'd Written

by Allison Moorer

MY SISTER, SHELBY LYNNE, and I both sang as soon as or maybe even before we could talk. I hung out around the piano and sang parts with our mama and grandmother's singing group by the time I was three. Daddy put Shelby on top of a table at Shakey's Pizza Parlor in Mobile, Alabama, to sing with the house band (she did Dean Martin's "Five Foot Two, Eyes of Blue") before I was born. I don't even know when we started singing together; neither of us remembers a time when we didn't.

Decades later, Shelby and I made our first album together. In the summer of 2016, we recorded songs written by other writers, save for one original we composed jointly through emails and recordings traded from opposite coasts. We could've chosen a thousand different songs to capture our moment, but not just any thousand songs. Without writing the record and having complete control of the structure of the tunes, which is what we're both used to doing, we still had to find a narrative and arc. We didn't want to just assemble a conglomeration that made no sense. This collection had to tell the listener who we are together, and take the shape of a story with a beginning, a middle, and an end.

We were well aware, of course, that most people approach intimacy with trepidation. We want to be known, but we're uncomfortable with too much conscious revealing. Personal revelations, however, are the songwriter's currency — the only tangible bits with which she can fumble to provide what a listener is looking for. Make no mistake; the listener is always looking for himself.

Of course, sometimes the listener is an artist too. More often than they like to admit, most songwriters will hear another writer's tune for the first time and feel jealousy creeping up their spine like liquid kudzu, leaving a hot, prickly trail of tongue-tied wanting. That particular sort of envy usually leads one of two places — to an instrument with pen and paper in hand or to the list of songs we keep tucked away in the back of our minds that we'd like to cover someday. Most of us who have those lists know they are long and ever evolving.

As Shelby said, "We had to decide really quickly if something wasn't going to cut it and move on to what we knew would. What [songs] we did [were] what we knew was solid and strong."

What was solid and strong in our case was what we know best — Merle Haggard's "Silver Wings," The Louvin Brothers' "Every Time You Leave," Jessi Colter's "I'm Looking for Blue Eyes" — the songs we grew up on. The Colter tune wasn't even on the list at first, but as we sat together in Shelby's living-room-turned-studio on the last day of recording, after the band had gone home but the tape was still rolling for us to do some songs on our own, it emerged like the magical old friend it is and insisted on being included; Shelby suggested that I sing it. We both recall the compilation album, *Wanted! The Outlaws*, with that song playing almost constantly in our house during the 1970s. "Blue Eyes" was also the very first song I learned to sing by myself and just about the only one on which Shelby would sing harmony instead of lead. I'm glad she didn't let me get away with not doing it on this record. To leave it off would've left out that part of our story.

We didn't want to only look behind us. Also included on *Not Dark Yet* are songs that we didn't know as well as the ones brought forth from our childhoods. We both submitted fresh ideas to the list we worked from as we neared our recording date — Shelby offered Nick Cave's "Into My Arms" and Nirvana's

We were raised on sad songs, songs that show you how to deal with grief and misery by exposing the common denominator of heartbreak. To turn away from those songs is to turn away from that part of art, is to turn away from that part of life.

"Lithium," and I threw in Townes Van Zandt's "Lungs." Disparate styles, maybe, but similar in that they are all some sort of narrow-eyed bids for salvation and grace. It's curious to find that thread now because my sister and I never talked about God being part of our record. However, there God is, hovering as we combine voices and spirits and find the buzz that only similar vocal cords working together can make.

Also hovering is what I think quickly became the through line for the story — almighty and elusive empathy. To be empathic is to understand and share feelings, yes, but for the two of us, there's another level entirely. This album is about our relationship, and the songs we chose reflect that, even though we never talked about that being its design.

Yes, we share DNA. We have the same vocal timbre, influences, mostly the same likes and dislikes, even some personality traits in common. But we also share history, the bonds of family and trauma, sometimes grandiose and wild experience, and collective memory that is stronger than even our bond of blood. Songs have always been our reference for almost everything. There hasn't been a moment in my life that I can recall not knowing who Merle Haggard was, so the devastating "Silver Wings" had to be included. We used to

sing that song with our parents when we were little girls. Sometimes I think it — as well as other songs, like "Every Time You Leave" — served as a study guide that we're still using for life.

We were raised on sad songs, songs that show you how to deal with grief and misery by exposing the common denominator of heartbreak. To turn away from those songs is to turn away from that part of art, is to turn away from that part of life. Of course, this album was always going to be full of tearjerkers. Singing tearjerkers is both our stock in trade and part of who we are not only as artists but also as women. Neither of us has ever shied away from the sad parts. You could argue that we've sometimes reveled in gloom, but also that we've had no choice in the matter. We've relied on songs and singing to simultaneously throw a lifeline to ourselves and to an audience that gravitated toward us and might need to know that they're not alone. On *Not Dark Yet*, we finally sing to each other.

Sounds Like Us

I first heard The Killers' "My List" at the end of a television show I'd been watching and it struck me as a song about a relationship that is carved in stone the way ours is. I put it on the song

list, knowing it was a must for me, and asked Shelby to consider it. It took her a while to warm to it, but after I showed her how it could work on an acoustic guitar and she understood how I interpreted it, it became one of her favorites. She'll never not know now that the first time I heard it, I thought of her.

By the same token, "Not Dark Yet" is a song that I've always felt speaks directly for us and to us somehow, thanks to the omniscience of Bob Dylan. The personality that emerges from it seems centered around a beaten-up stoicism that can only come with the resigned exhale of knowing things fall apart and that you find a way to live through the crumbling, until you don't. At its center is irregularly shaped hope and a reserved, yet almost appreciative, nod toward life experience. Surrounding that hope and appreciation is weariness and fragile, worn-thin resilience. It's a song that sounds like us to me. You can feel us intuiting each other as we trade verses and underscore the emotion on the lines we feel like sharing.

Empathy doesn't come from just imagining yourself in another's shoes and contemplating how they feel, but rather through considering the happenings in their life and how those things add up to who they are at present. Then you must cogitate how the other

Shelby Lynne, left, and Allison Moorer.

person navigates the world with the filter of their experience. It's a tall order that deep-rooted familiarity makes easier. Indeed, my sister knows more about what I carry than anyone else on the planet, and vice versa.

When we did pick up our pens for the very last track, "Is It Too Much," we found ourselves exploring our thorough knowledge of the emotional heaviness we both shoulder, but also inviting the other to give it up.

Bring it here to my side,
Tell me about the tears you've cried
Lord knows you must be tired by now
Whisper what you never tell,
Don't you know you ain't by yourself
I'm right here to help you lay it down.

My sister and I have always tried to carry each other, but now it seems we have greater understanding of how we might pull that off — by listening as closely as possible. Music is something we don't have to talk about, so we talk about everything else through it, whether we have the conversation by singing our own songs or those by other writers with which we identify and find pieces of ourselves. We never had to discuss what we liked about Jason Isbell and Amanda Shires' "The Color of a Cloudy Day," we just agreed it was a must upon our first listen. It's a song that I wish I'd written, and I'd bet she does too.

Singing is emotional shorthand and expresses what speaking can't even touch. You can hear us reaching toward

each other on this set of songs, and whether or not we wrote them doesn't really matter, except that sometimes a cover can expose a singer even more than an original can — our taste and what we connect with goes a long way toward disclosing who we are. On *Not Dark Yet*, my sister and I find each other through our marrow-deep consciousness — dipping and diving, wavering and solidifying according to the other's vocal movements — because we want to provide sturdiness and balance, and that's the best, most natural way we know how to do it. This record is, above all, filled with songs that allow us to discover that kind of revelation, that kind of irrepressible humanity, and that kind of love. ∎

DANGER AND HIGH ROMANCE

Josh Ritter on exploring the world through songwriting

by Erin Lyndal Martin

JOSH RITTER ONCE TOLD AN interviewer from *American Songwriter*, "Don't ever try to write a hit." Indeed, Ritter will probably never write one. He tends to write love songs about such obscure subjects as mummies, nuclear warheads, and the orbital decay of stars. Yet he has amassed a steadfast fanbase that appreciates the unflinching focus he puts on his craft. Among them is *Paste* magazine, who named Ritter one of the 100 Greatest Living Songwriters when he was only 30. (He's now 41.) Stephen King is a fan too — he wrote that Ritter's 2006 song "Thin Blue Flame," was the "most exuberant outburst of imagery since Bob Dylan's 'A Hard Rain's A-Gonna Fall.'"

Alongside Ritter's prolific and sharply honed songwriting, he has expanded his prowess to other arenas. In 2011, he published his first novel, *Bright's Passage*, which chronicles a returning World War I veteran's mystical and grueling journey across Appalachia. Even as he was writing songs for his latest album, this year's *Gathering*, Ritter had returned to painting and allowed his artwork and songwriting to cross-pollinate. In an essay for NPR Music, he wrote that the album's songs began with an "exciting sense of dissatisfaction" that moved him to write and record more songs than he'd ever had for an album before. He went on to note that he felt like he's been living in the shadow of the songs he's written over the past 20 years.

Objectively, it was the earlier work that brought him here, to a fertile place of exciting dissatisfaction and an audience eagerly awaiting the fruits of it.

In a recent interview, Ritter and I discussed many of these things, including love songs, autobiographical songwriting, and the importance of setting goals. Our conversation has been edited for length and continuity.

ERIN LYNDAL MARTIN: Do you remember the first song you ever wrote?

JOSH RITTER: Yes, I do. I don't remember what song it was, but I remember the writing. I remember that it felt like a miracle to me, because I was a kid in high school who couldn't do anything. I wasn't particularly very good at school, I wasn't good at sports, I had none of the things that would make a name for [me] and

> **"To limit expression to the confines of our own experience is to artificially limit the scope of our art. Writing is a chance to explore the vastness of human nature and possibility.**
> **Why only walk in our own footsteps?"**
>
> Josh Ritter .

give me my own identity. Suddenly I discovered songs. I discovered the D chord, and the D chord worked with the G chord, and I wrote a song.

I sat on the edge of my bed in my parents' house and the whole thing unfolded like magic. Suddenly I had my thing. I remember that so well. I have a vague memory of some of the songs I wrote at the time, but I couldn't tell you which one it was. I was already kind of falling down the rabbit hole with writing.

ELM: I was thinking about your songs, "The Temptation of Adam" and "The Curse." You have these nontraditional settings for romance and you manage to make them very moving. Is there something that you feel makes a love song effective, or are you just telling a story that happens to work on that level?

JR: It's a little bit of [both]. There's a great deal of luck that goes into a song like "The Temptation of Adam," where somehow the whole thing ties itself in a bow at the end. There's the skill in the writing, but [also] the luck of finding the story.

There's so many different types [of love songs]. There's the kind of biblical, very high, ornate language that can be beautiful. ... [There's] the depth and passion that's there, like Shakespeare

sonnets, where there can be spite, but [where] love is like every color, it absorbs everything. There's room for humor in there, and there's room for sadness and sorrow and happiness, and the quizzical aspect of love.

In the end, love is not a single thing. It's not like the monolith in *2001[: A Space Odyssey]*. It's a whole bunch of different things, a whole bunch of different shades of things. So to [write] an honest love song, to feel like it actually has love involved, it can't just be like "I love you, I love you, I love you." It has to be "I love you. Remember when this happened, remember when we made it through this, remember these things?"

There are some great love songs about couples crossing the street, but my type tends to be a little bit more fraught. I feel like if I could write a straight love song, I could retire. I can't figure it out.

ELM: A lot of writers have different metaphors for what the writing process is like for them. What's yours?

JR: I think about it like my audience allows me to be an explorer. It gives me the tools and the resources I need to go out and cut myself free from a lot of things so that I can work on exploring ... my preoccupations and turning them into work.

When you discover a song, when you discover a new style of writing or a new approach, [you're] discovering a continent that's all yours. That's what makes it so exciting — the process of discovering and the journey toward that, which can be frustrating and fraught with danger and high romance.

ELM: Every song is different, but do you have a handful of tricks you go to when you get stuck in your writing process?

JR: My tricks are different now than they used to be. Before I had a kid, and my time was fully my own, I would put the guitar away and I would sit down and watch a movie. I would do something fun like that, something to loosen up the brain. These days, I take a little piece of that song with me and I write in my head wherever I am. I compose the lyrics in my mind and I hold on to them as much as I can until I can get them on paper.

I've [gotten] out of the stage where I'm staring at the paper all the time, and I've moved on to not always needing the paper. I'll carry these verses around in my head until later, when I can actually have the chance to write them down. Stuff can occur to you anywhere, even when you don't have your pen and paper around, so I can walk around and leave a song and I know something will come to me. That's kind of my big trick.

The other thing is that it's hard to put down a song when it's not working. It's hard to let it go. There's no trick to letting go of something that's been frustrating you all morning; you just have to do it.

ELM: How else has your writing process changed over the years?

JR: Every time I write a song it feels different. When you walk through a door, it's a very simple thing: you open the door and walk through, but nobody walks through the door [the same way] twice. You walk in the door, it's a little bit different every time, whether you're holding the door open for somebody, or you knock, or you open the locked side, or you push and it doesn't open, or you pull and it doesn't. It's like that. But once you're through the door, you're through. You don't think about it.

I feel like that's exactly how writing is. You're looking for a way in, but once you're in, you don't have any idea how you got there.

I don't know that my style has changed over the years of writing, and my method of writing hasn't changed over time. I've become a little bit more used to the idea that it's going to happen a little differently every time. As soon as I start to come up with reasons why I

should do something before I write, I feel like it's superstitious.

ELM: What role does editing play for you? Are you somebody who edits things a lot, or does it all depend on the song, or do you like to leave it as it came out?

JR: I believe that a really good idea deserves really good editing. I'm not a believer in the genius of a song written without an edit. I think that can happen on rare occasions, but I don't think that's the way to treat an idea.

When I am done with a song, I'm done. I've been editing the whole way. It's gone through five permutations, and when it's done, that's [it]. I circle it on the page and I move on to the second verse. So when you are finally done, you have, like, 15 pages of edited material that has five verses. When I'm done, I've edited like crazy.

ELM: You've said that you always disliked autobiography in songwriting. Why is that?

JR: I dislike autobiography at the exclusion of all else. It's important to be able to speak directly about one's own life and feelings. It's one of the main reasons people get into writing songs. However, to limit expression to the confines of our own experience is to artificially limit the scope of our art. Writing is a chance to

explore the vastness of human nature and possibility. Why only walk in our own footsteps?

ELM: Your 2013 album *The Beast in Its Tracks* is unusual for you in how autobiographical and straightforward its lyrics are. Did making and releasing that album change anything for you as a songwriter?

JR: It gave me the realization that sometimes cold, realistic description is as effective as any imaginative flight. With *Beast*, I was trying to be as plainspoken about heartbreak and new love as I could. It meant for once holding up a mirror to my own hopes and fears and describing them as plainly as I could. It was a new muscle to flex, and it was vital to the making of the record.

ELM: When you write, do you have your guitar in your arms at the same time or is writing usually separate from the instrument? Or a mixture of both?

JR: I usually start with the guitar. There's a way I think about it that's like, I have these ideas or these phrases or even these words that kind of stick around in my brain, and the guitar is the other half of that. There are chord progressions and riffs that are kind of flying around in there, and I pick them up and I kind of bash the two together, and I wait for

"Write about whatever you want. There's nothing wrong in writing. Whatever you made, it never existed before and it's there for a purpose."

Josh Ritter

something to fit. It's not scientific.

When inspiration strikes it's usually because these two pieces of things fit together in a way that feels effortless, like when a puzzle piece actually fits. ... I really like to get the pieces to fit together effortlessly, so I have the guitar with me a lot of the time, and then oftentimes, once I have the pattern situated, I put it down. I just concentrate solely on the writing once the rhythm of the words is in my head. I find that just holding the guitar makes it hard to write.

ELM: Do you ever find yourself writing songs that you don't think you could pull off as a performer?

JR: I find that performance and writing are so interconnected that I never write without partially thinking about the audience. There's an elasticity to the space in between the performer and the audience. The content, length, and situation of the song [with]in the set all play a part in how the song is presented and received. I only write songs that I can pull off, but that sometimes means expanding as a performer to accommodate the song.

ELM: They say that writers are either putter-inners or taker-outers. Which one are you?

JR: You've got to wear both hats as a writer. Songs are like those bridges kids make out of toothpicks. They're a fragile structure and can easily fall apart. They can only exist in perfect balance with themselves, so there's always a process of putting in and taking out until the whole thing hangs together as elegantly and as sturdily as possible.

ELM: Sometimes, when I'm working on poetry or fiction, I have other authors' books that are templates or instructional to what I'm doing. Did you have any authors or books that were influential for *Bright's Passage*?

JR: Definitely. *Paris Trout* by Pete Dexter was a big one for me. Muriel Spark, almost anything by Muriel Spark. Those books are full of concision. They told stories in a concise way. There's a really dark humor in them and they felt like short little sonatas where you could fall into and reread, and those were so cool.

I always loved A.S. Byatt, with her incredible use of language. And there were a lot of nonfiction [books] that took me into the infinite world of the early 20th century. Barbara Tuchman, who's a phenomenal writer. She's a big one for me.

ELM: How do you feel that your songwriting experience helped you to write a novel?

JR: I'd say that novel writing helped me in the rest of my life. Songwriting is something you that you can write and write, and, if you're lucky, in an afternoon you can have a song that didn't exist before that. With a novel, you have to be patient. You have to work all day on something to get a few pages and have, in essence, nothing to show. The pages pile up over time, and that really has always been a touchstone for larger projects and larger goals in my life: It's going to take me a while, but I'm going to start now, and I'll put the shovel down today and pick it back up again tomorrow. In that

way it's been incredibly important in my life.

ELM: What advice would you give to songwriters who are maybe just getting started?

JR: I would say, know what you're doing it for. If you're writing songs because it just makes you happy, then you're blessed.

Write about whatever you want. There's nothing wrong in writing. Whatever you made, it never existed before and it's there for a purpose. So to people who are songwriters, who are wanting to make their career doing music, I would say ... learn a sense of perspective — where am I in my career, how do I appreciate where I am, and what goals do I make for myself that will bring me to the next level where I can get more people to hear my music, so that I can try to make a living? I can't overstate the power of having goals.

A lot of music, the story of the music and the stories that we're told about our heroes is that their talent was so undeniable that there was no chance they wouldn't be found and turned into rock gods. The fact is, all of these people started off in their garages playing for themselves and just had a dream to be someone, to be something, with their music, and they worked really hard for that. I think it's a really destructive idea that our heroes didn't start someplace, they were born sui generis.

So be proud of who you are, be proud of the songs you're writing, and if you're not satisfied, figure out what's not satisfying you and then fix it. ∎

Eye of the beholder

For a solo singer-songwriter, touring around the world can be both a soul-feeding and deeply lonesome experience. You encounter kind strangers and absurd moments everywhere you go. There's always something beautiful or funny, if you're looking. Then again, most cities look and feel basically the same as you roll in, set up, sound check, play the show, and leave. Sometimes these dichotomies find their way into songs — the sheer amount of songs that have been written about being on the road, missing loved ones, wondering where one's roots are, and watching the miles tick by attest to this. But much of a songwriter's life is simply absorbed as it slowly, incrementally changes them. Some songwriters turn this absorbed energy into novels or paintings; Rose Cousins turns it into photography.

Based in Halifax, Nova Scotia, Cousins writes the kind of songs that pour through tears. "I don't know that I have what it takes to be chosen," she sings on the opening song from her latest release, *Natural Conclusion,* released earlier this year. And in a way, that uncertainty drives so much of her intensely personal lyrics on all of her eight albums. Behind the lyrics, she gently strums a guitar or moves through progressions on a piano, the music enveloping and supporting her words like water under a raft, the writer adrift. Her songs' precarious balance of melancholy and hope is arresting. It's like you can feel the cool air off the coast of her native Prince Edward Island, and how it must have shaped her creative unconscious.

These things also come through in her photography — a craft she has quietly honed offstage even as her music has won her attention and awards. In these pages, she shares 20 photographs that capture the moods and moments of a single year on the road, traveling with friends and alone, opening for stars like Mary Chapin Carpenter and sailing through Canada on a coast guard vessel, past icebergs and Native communities. There are several small moments of beauty and connection, and others where one wonders how to pass from one moment to the next. I could write many words about her exquisite music-making, but her photography says so much more.

— *Kim Ruehl*

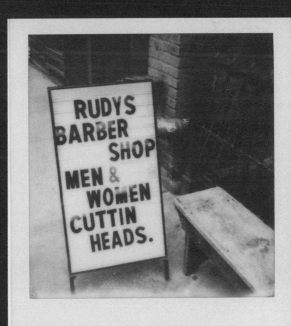

IN HARMONY

Jolie Holland and Samantha Parton reunite for "Wildflower Blues"

by John Kruth

The unexpected reunion of Jolie Holland and Samantha Parton, two founding members of the Be Good Tanyas, is a reason for joy in these challenging and uncertain times. While they are both fine singers and songwriters in their own right, together they embody what the gentleman junkie scribe William S. Burroughs once dubbed the "Third Mind," writing emotionally compelling songs and weaving luscious magnolia-breeze harmonies that make your temperature flush. Their new album, *Wildflower Blues*, is gorgeous stuff, between Holland's disembodied siren blues and Parton's warm-heart whisper, and behind them a fine band conjures the perfect sonic atmosphere.

"It's all kinds of a dream come true to do this," Holland enthused in a recent interview. "It's an honor to play and sing with Sam. When we were mixing the album at Jackpot studios in Portland, the engineer, Larry Crane, used an iZotope RX, a very useful tool which cleans up tracks to an amazingly fine degree. Larry had also worked on my [2014] album, *Wine Dark Sea,* and the iZotope made a visual spectrum of soundwaves that looked like the colors of fire, like the blue flames on a stovetop on the bottom with yellow/white on top. Looking at our voices on that program, you could literally see my tone was hard and precise while Sam's voice is breathy and diffuse. I wish I'd taken a picture of it, it was so beautiful."

Beyond the beauty of technology, *Wildflower Blues* is an honest document, full of sounds so warm you'd swear there was a glowing campfire in the middle of the studio while they cut these tunes. The band features guitarist/harmony vocalist Stevie Weinstein-Foner's ragged, jagged guitar solos, Jared Samuel's trilling piano blues, and Justin Veloso's intuitive drumming, while Holland's box fiddle possesses more homemade natural distortion than any acoustic instrument I've ever heard. Handmade by her friend Stefan Jecusco, the instrument has a distinctive tone that alternates from a feral growl to an eerie banshee wail with one stroke of the bow.

Back in the day, when your favorite artist released a new album, the ritual involved deliberately making space in your life to dedicate your full attention to the first couple of listenings. You didn't multitask. You didn't answer the phone. You settled down in your favorite chair or laid across your bed and gave yourself fully to the experience. It was an important missive worthy of your time and concentration. This is definitely one of those kind of records.

It opens with Townes Van Zandt's regretful ballad "You Are Not Needed Now," penned by the late, great Texas troubadour in memory of Janis Joplin.

"It was the first take of the first song for the album," says Parton. "It was pretty clear right from the start that magic was afoot. I was blown away by Jolie's vocal. It's like an incantation."

"The song is a meta-Texan experience, written about a Texan by a Texan and reinterpreted by a Texan," Holland points out. "Stevie and I were singing it before I started the band with Sam. It's more soul-searching and kind than Leonard Cohen's song 'Chelsea Hotel' was about Janis. And it's a great vehicle for harmonies, with all those choruses."

Next, Parton loans some heavy-lidded, boozy vocals to the title track, "Wildflower Blues," an understated, feelin'-no-pain blues shuffle with a shot of Bob Dylan's cold and lonely, impeccably written "Meet Me in the Morning" thrown in for good measure.

"There's a J.J. Cale thing to that song," Parton says. "I didn't write it with him in mind, but [I] recorded it with him in mind. I had a longstanding fantasy to go to Tulsa and drive around until I found his house and sit on the porch and have a little jam with him."

The song's lyrical imagery is rich and sweeping.

Summer breeze a blowin'
storm coming in
gonna stand on a mountain
throw my petals to the wind.

It's a timeless verse that evokes the ageless folk poetry of old blues tunes by Mississippi John Hurt and Mance Lipscomb.

I'm a wildflower and I'm growing
like a weed
all the bees come down from
heaven, make honey outta me.

"It's kind of a kiss-off song," Parton admits. "But it's also a celebration of finding strength through vulnerability."

Out of the Wilderness

Parton, whose ethereal vocals reveal a tender soul, has had no choice but to toughen up in recent years, as a matter of survival. A pair of back-to-back car accidents in 2012 and 2013, followed by brain surgery for an aneurysm behind her eye, took her off the road with the Tanyas and led to several years of downtime as she struggled to cope with chronic pain and other issues.

"When Jolie called me and asked me to make an album with her, I was kind of in the wilderness," she says. "I was struggling to play my instruments, struggling to connect with my creativity. I was worried about not being able to step up. But I also knew I could trust Jolie to understand where I was at and work with that, so I said yes."

Holland decamped to Vancouver, British Columbia, and the two began squeezing writing sessions into Parton's schedule. "Sam has a little downstairs studio apartment she calls 'The Cabin.' It has a sweet vibe to it," says Holland. "I was working on the songs full time. Sam was busy working and going to doctors. Then she'd come work with me for as long as she could, and eventually we got a bunch of songs written."

"Partnerships and friendships have their own rhythm," Parton adds. "Sometimes they're like satellites. The timing of Jolie's return in my life was so meaningful. ... I had been quite isolated, and the Be Good Tanyas had carried on without me, which was understandable, but also really difficult. Jolie brought this real loving encouragement into my world. It's a healing feeling when someone is with you, supports you and believes in you. I feel like the universe brought us back together."

One of the songs they penned together during those sessions was the soulful ballad "Make It Up to Me," a song they hoped to give to Sharon Jones, who sadly passed away shortly after the demo was recorded. "It was one of those magic, out-of-thin-air songs," says Parton. "We knew what we wanted to say and where we wanted to go with it, and really fed off of each other's ideas as we were writing."

Later on the disc, like a gentle, rolling Mississippi John Hurt tune, propelled by Justin Veloso's drums, Parton paints the bucolic fantasy "Little Black Bear," who shows up at her "little cabin, way back in the pines" with "honey on his mind." Lonely, beneath a cold moon, an invitation "to light a little fire," is soon offered, and what happens next ... is left up to the listener.

At some point while listening to "Little Black Bear," I began to drift off. Not because I was bored or from the usual lack of sleep, but due to the song's

Jolie Holland, left, and Samantha Parton.

"I joke to people about this band, that I get to live out my fantasy of being in the Trio band that Dolly Parton, Emmylou Harris, and Linda Ronstadt had in the '80s," jokes Weinstein-Foner. "I'm not sure which one I am, though — maybe Linda?

"Jolie and Sam both have really iconic voices, each with their own unique sound," he adds. "And Sam is an incredible harmony singer. I really love singing harmonies, and she and I have had a great time writing the parts for these songs. When Jolie brought 'The Last' to us, she said she imagined Byrds-style harmonies. Sam and I were able to find them immediately.

"In the studio, Samantha can be like an impressionist painter with harmonies, finding infinite variations, each of which communicate a slightly different nuance or subtlety of the line or song, whereas I sort of have an idea of what the part is and don't stray too far from that unless I have to," he continues. "What I've found with singing with both Jolie and Sam is that I have to be really, really listening, because they each have

wistful lilt, which transported me to another place, the crack between the worlds, as a Taos shaman I once knew used to say. And in those few suspended moments, I had a fleeting dream that Parton had married a bear. When I told her this, she laughed. "A lot of old folklore has women marrying bears. That song kind of has to do with a feeling of loneliness, and the many years I spent living in the bush, working as a tree-planter in British Columbia. I loved the idea of wilderness, but found it

all quite vast and lonely, and longed for a house in the city, with good neighbors, a good partner, and strong community, even as I longed for solitude, and a cabin in the woods all to myself."

Following the Flow

Making a great record is all about chemistry, and choosing the right people to record and perform with. It's rare when band members openly appreciate each other like this bunch.

"The beautiful thing was our implicit trust and respecting each other's opinions, and making the songs the best they can be. You have to have that person you can go to."

Jolie Holland

such unique voices and phrasing. Every song, every line, will be slightly different every time we sing it, and in order to keep the song a living, breathing thing, I've got to stay with the pulse of it instead of just assuming I know how it goes. The two of them have been singing together for so long that they have a real sense of each others' voices and rhythms. At their best, they are tapped into the same mind and flow of a song. So, for me it's been an attempt to tap into that flow."

Parton appreciates what he brings to that flow, though she recognizes "it's unusual to have a male voice supporting two female singers. But [Stevie] has such a magical voice, an impeccable sense of harmony, and a soulful touch on the guitar. He is 'Mr. Serve the Song,' which I really appreciate. He has no ego. He's been a really important part of the project, all the way through."

Indeed, a soulful choir comprised of Holland, Parton, and Weinstein-Foner testifies in their remake of Dylan's "Minstrel Boy," which plods along like a loose-jointed funeral march. Ever the imaginative songwriter, Holland adds a

couple of new faces to the gallery of ragged characters that inhabit the frontier town of Dylan's imagination — that elusive twist in the road that author Greil Marcus once dubbed "Old, Weird America." Formerly the domain of Lucky, the Sisyphean truck driver, forever struggling to hump his old wreck over the hill, Holland's version of Dylan's song now includes the specter of Jesse (the poet Steven Jesse Bernstein) with his tattooed fingers crossing that "tall trestle bridge" that links the two worlds. Next, we're introduced to Billy (short for William Blake), singing his radiant ditties in dirty old Londontown, backed by a choir of "eternal angels." Holland's love of Blake's ethereal verse reappears throughout the album as she evokes his "Lion and the Tyger lying down with the Lamb," vowing (as we've heard from everyone from Blake to Sister Rosetta Tharp) to meet him "next year in Jerusalem."

And the songwriting just gets more creative the further you go into the album. While the title of the track "Johnny Said to May" evokes the old

murder ballad "Frankie and Johnnie," the song itself is a spiritual meditation on love. Holland's voice is one of pure yearning while the drums roll and crash like turbulent waves that rise higher and higher, creating the sonic equivalent of an El Greco painting, a modern-day soundtrack for those awaiting Judgment Day.

"The song was already more than half done when I showed it to Sam," notes Holland, offering some backstory. "I wasn't sure if it was even a song. But the beautiful thing was our implicit trust and respecting each other's opinions, and making the songs the best they can be. You have to have that person you can go to. We trust each other enough to show the works in progress. It takes the right person to see that."

Like the artists' collaboration, *Wildflower Blues* might not answer all the questions currently nagging your soul, but if you let Holland and Parton's ephemeral vocals fall gently on your heart, the world might make a bit more sense and even seem like a friendlier place — at for least a little while. ∎

THERE WILL BE DANCING

Discussing joy, sorrow, politics, and songwriting

"I'm the shepherd and the words are my flock, and I take care of them and out they come. But I do have to commit myself to the discipline of writing."

Emily Saliers

TO BE A GREAT SONGWRITER is, necessarily, to wear your heart on your sleeve. You must summon the courage to lay it all on the line — the heartache and the hope, the virtues and the vices. The same necessity could be applied to being a queer woman in the world. Your mere presence among the heteronormative masses turns even the most personal struggle into a political issue. When you claim both of those identities, the only way out of your own bubble is through the vulnerability that could easily burst it all wide open.

Which is just fine by both Emily Saliers and Chastity Brown. Each stands firmly, fiercely, and faithfully in those identities, as well as several others: person of color, activist, Southerner, seeker, daughter, mother, friend, wife, and partner among them. Some of those identities intersect cleanly with the world-at-large; some don't. But they all play a part in serving the songs that Saliers and Brown create.

After 30 years as one-half of the Indigo Girls, Saliers finally stepped out with an album of her own, this year's *Murmuration Nation*. On it, she explores not only the various psychological facets of her self, but the various musical aspects as well. Though she's best-known as a folksinger, despite railing against that label internally, she's also an artistic adventurer, as this album shows. Similarly, ten years and five albums into her career, Brown wields an acoustic guitar and harmonica, folding non-folk influences and elements into her work, as well, on this year's *Silhouette of Sirens*. Putting them in conversation with each other evidences how we often have more in common with someone than not. The conversation has been edited for length and clarity.

KELLY McCARTNEY: What approach do each of you take when it comes to songwriting? Do you write the songs or do the songs write themselves through you?

EMILY SALIERS: It's a combination of both. I'm the channeler of the song. I can't say that it's all just magic and mystery and I have nothing to do with it, obviously, because I have to sit at my desk. I have to scoop out the time. I have to focus on putting words together. But there's a lot of alchemy that happens in songwriting. For instance, I may write a line in a song that has a double or triple meaning that I didn't even intend. ... I said the line because it's at least one thing that I intend [to say]. ... Other times, I write lines in a song that have a life of their own [and] I cannot attribute that to me, so there's a little bit of that magic and channeling going [on].

I really believe that music is such a powerful force in life and nobody really owns it, so we're kind of like shepherds. I'm the shepherd and the words are my flock, and I take care of them and out they come. But I do have to commit myself to the discipline of writing.

CHASTITY BROWN: I like what you said about the double or triple meaning. I just released an album a few months ago, and I find myself in interviews. Each time I'm talking about a song, I'll talk about it from a different perspective. Someone will say, "In this previous interview, you said the song was about this." And it's like, "Yeah, it *was*, and it *is*, however ... "

I can pinpoint parts of it that were personal, but there's a transference of energy and it evolves into something more palpable, and it's no longer about [what I started writing about]. So I appreciate you saying that, Emily.

There is a mysterious quality to [songs]. If I'm trying to write a song and it's not coming, I find myself begging it, as though it were a woman or a muse, "Please just talk to me. What can I do to coerce you into coming out?"

ES: Oh, my God. I'm going to try that next time! I've never tried that!

CB: Then, other times, there are songs I feel like I try to run away from — the songs that really get me in the gut that are heartbreaking. There have been times when it's like, "I don't want to write you. I don't want to go there." Inevitably, I end up writing it, but there are times when I feel like I'm being chased by the song and I'm like, "No. Please. Go easy on me!"

ES: It's interesting that you say that. Now, I write more like a discipline. I'm going to use the word "job." It's difficult and it can be agonizing, but it's not tedious. But I often feel, when I haven't written and I sit down to write, I'll just start writing. I haven't even constructed anything solid yet and I'll get a lump in my throat and I'll start crying. I don't know if that ever happens to you, Chastity.

CB: Yeah.

ES: But it's like you're giving the well the permission to open up and flow over. No one's in the room, unless you're co-writing, so you're vulnerable, but only to yourself. When you talk about how you don't want to write that song or you don't feel like getting into that, it's because it's raw. I find that, unless I'm writing a pop song for fun or for relief, that rawness is always emotional for me.

CB: I agree. ... I'm not religious, but I did grow up in Tennessee, [in the] Southern gospel church, where music

Emily Saliers

> **"We need to be dancing right now, because there's so much pain. … I love Alice Walker, and she says, 'Where there's tears there will be dancing.' It's the only counter-alternative."**
>
> Chastity Brown

takes over the service. I remember when I was learning about praise and worship, my mentor said, "You can't take people where you've never gone." Even though I'm not religious anymore, I am quite spiritual and I still feel that way. If [a song] brings me to that point, I think that [it will] enable me to take the listener to that point. If I'm not willing to go there, even if it's a fucking rock-out jam, if I don't allow myself to go full-throttle, then how in the world will a listener be able to do that?

Honestly, where I am, at my stage of songwriting, it's really incredible to hear from you, Emily, that you're still humbled by the song, that there's still that thing that gets you.

ES: More than ever, I think. We never know when we're going to "go," but statistically speaking, I'm not in my twilight. In middle age, I've just started to absorb the world differently, and now that I have a child, that [adds to] it as well.

But speaking about Southern gospel, I grew up in the church. My dad is a theologian. He was progressive, so there was nothing in my organized religion experience that ever throttled me or judged me, as it came through my parents. I was fortunate in that way. Now, of course, I have a huge struggle with the Methodist church because they will not change their language that homosexuality is incompatible with the teachings of Christ, which, to me, is bullshit.

I grew up in Atlanta, but I was born in New Haven. And, in New Haven, we lived in a predominantly African-American neighborhood and there was lots of gospel, soul, and R&B music. That is the music of my heart and soul. So, when we moved down to Atlanta, you've got the Ebenezer Baptist Church and you have black American gospel music everywhere in the life of the city and the communities. That, to me, is my straight path to — I'll call it "God" — my spiritual source. I attribute … everything to that spiritual source. Music like that, the words are of the head but the music and the spirit is of the body.

I've got to get out of my own head. I don't know about you, but when I'm most free, I'm in my body and my head at the same time. That's what that gospel music does to me. In fact, that's what I tried to do a little bit on my solo record — get a rhythm section to express the songs in a way I hadn't done, historically, with Indigo Girls.

CB: I love that. That's one thing I say that I learned in the gospel church: to sing from your gut.

Sometimes church music would last two or three hours … because I grew up in a Pentecostal church. I went to seminary school in Baltimore, but I was kicked out for dating a woman. So that was my dramatic departure from organized religion, but it's still so dear to me.

But singing from your gut — I didn't realize that was what I was learning. I also didn't realize I was learning how to harmonize. Harmony just makes sense to me [now], but only because I grew up with people constantly singing four and five parts. In the church, you have permission to sing exactly how you feel, or to try to excavate how you feel and get all that shit out.

KM: If the church and gospel music taught you how to excavate your emotions through your physical voice, what of your lyrical voice? Do you give yourself permission to go wherever you need to? And is there a difference in the level of vulnerability that either of you feels in writing confessional form versus writing in story form?

ES: I don't have any problem going as honest and as deep and as painful [as I can] in my lyrics. Some of my old songs, I look at and go, "Oh, man. You should've just closed your mouth when you had a chance!" But for me, the vulnerability [comes] when I sit down to write and this well opens up, and I get super emotional and I haven't even created anything yet or channeled anything yet.

As far as the content of a song, I never shut anything down. The only thing I ever did, or have done historically, is not pick on people, especially to the point where they might recognize themselves in a song. In that sense, there have been times when I wanted to vent about a personal thing, but out of respect, I can't be that honest.

KM: Do you ever couch that in a story, though, so that you can put a spin on it and still process it?

ES: I don't really think of myself as a story-song writer. I feel much more confessional. How about you, Chastity?

CB: I feel like it's both, at the same time. It's so difficult to be objective. I do sometimes say that, in my most recent body of work, it's the first time [I've been] brave enough to be truly vulnerable. It took me four years to get [this album] out because I just couldn't grapple with how vulnerable it made me feel.

At the same time, I feel like not all the stories are particularly about my personal life. They are stories I've lived and imagined. Still, some of these songs are about different types of heartbreak and trying to give light to a more proletariat, working-class experience of what it feels like to witness a loved one who struggles with mental health. That's not a type of heartbreak song that people generally write, but it's fucking heartbreaking and it's a common experience.

ES: I wish that I didn't care what people thought after a song was written. I don't think about people — fans, listeners, judgers, whatever — while I'm writing. But when it's done, I hate to admit that I need outside validation in different ways. Like, "Is this a good song?"

You know, Kelly ... I asked Amy [Ray], "Do you think Kelly likes my record?" It's like that. I'm not afraid to get vulnerable, like I said. I'll write anything. But there's all this other conflict about how I really want it to be received. I guess most artists have that.

But I also have the conflict of, "Ugh.

I'm a woman with an acoustic guitar. I'm emotional ... " And I get all those societal stereotypes wearing down my psyche: "You should be tough. You should be edgy. You should should should." That is where the vulnerability really eats at me. I still hope, at this point in my life and career, [that] it's getting a little better. But it's not that much better.

CB: That's one of my fears, as well: Am I going to just, once again, be pigeonholed like every other — not only just woman with an acoustic guitar — but a queer, black woman with an acoustic guitar? Man, I can *play*.

There's power, I think, in stabilizing the groups that I feel represent me. Sometimes, I'm like, "Oh, shit. Am I ostracizing people so severely that the common listener wouldn't want to listen?" But some of those people['s] political views are such that I wouldn't even want them at my shows. Or, maybe I would, and I would hope that maybe their hearts would be affected and they'd be provoked into empathy.

KM: Because you are both out, queer women, the political becomes the personal, in your songs and in your lives, and vice versa. Do either of you wish it were any other way?

CB: What's interesting to me is that I feel like I've never been exactly political. But until the past few years, I've been very outspoken about things I take very personally — women's reproductive rights, but even more, Black Lives Matter. It's so crazy to be a woman of color and publicly love myself. People

think that's political.

ES: I think "political" is a word that is used often, but it doesn't exactly paint the picture. I think more in terms of social change, rather than political. I use the word "political" all the time, but it's kind of like "spiritual" — what, exactly, does it mean to me as I say it? Politics, legislators, deal-making, deep state ... all that stuff.

When I think of taking action and being an activist, it's all for the purpose of social change and it's a very, very simple common denominator: Where there's suffering due to oppression — whatever the oppressor is, if it's privilege or race or access — I feel intrinsically that my relationship to the rest of my community and the world is to be a member and support the leaders and those who are taking part in social change to alleviate suffering. [That is] on fire right now in this country.

To answer your question, I wouldn't have it any other way. That is one thing I don't care about anymore. If I have any kind of political content in my songs, I don't care if it turns somebody off. I just go from how I feel and what serves me. It's all personal, but it ends up affecting the political.

The more people get fired up, personally, about injustice or social movements, the more it affects things and swings the pendulum back. We're in a terrible presidency right now, but things are largely the same for communities of color as they have been since slavery.

Chastity Brown

KM: It also becomes a crisis of faith — the political, the personal, the spiritual all get bundled up, in times like this, because justice is in every aspect of our lives.

ES: In that sense, I get overwhelmed. I read Twitter and I vote and I call my senators and I try to show up. But I get overwhelmed by the darkness.

When I see joy in my kid ... if I'm surrounded by goodness and light and frivolity, even NFL football — not the organization, but the game — the personal experience of there still being good people working for good things and we're still laughing, those are the only things that keep me from being completely depressed and detached from society, because [otherwise] I couldn't handle it.

KM: I keep thinking that music seems so frivolous, in times like this, on one hand. On the other hand, it seems like the only thing keeping many of us sane

and grounded and moving forward.

CB: I have a white partner and I'm half-white, and my mom is blond-haired, blue-eyed Irish, so I lie in bed sometimes and think about how white privilege affects my life. My partner will be like, "What's wrong?" And I'll say, "I'm just thinking about patriarchy and white privilege, even though it's 8 a.m. and I need to walk the dog."

On those days — and I'm not hugely into funk music — but lately I love the audacity of funk. After the most worldwide, public atrocities [against] black and brown people in the late '60s, then, in the '70s, funk [came] on the scene. It restores me. It makes me think of what's happening now. [But] everybody asks, "Are you writing protest songs? What have you written since Trump's election?" I've written some fucking love songs, because I also need to hear that right now.

As you were saying, Emily, about

your new album and dancing — hell yes. We need to be dancing right now because there's so much pain. I agree, it's overwhelming. I love Alice Walker, and she says, "Where there are tears, there will be dancing." It's the only counter-alternative.

ES: I have felt, at Indigo Girls shows since the election, the need for music and to sing out loud at the top of your lungs and be in a room of joyful songs. But, also, the embracing of the pain. The full human-ness. Societally, we're so afraid of that. Let's take a look at the full human-ness of what's going on.

Alice Walker is right with what she said. I've felt a palpable difference in the spirit of Indigo Girls shows in what people need. We just did the Four Voices tour with Joan Baez and Mary Chapin Carpenter. Oh my gosh. The power and the joy, but also allowing ourselves to feel pain, as well, communally. It's been very powerful.

KM: Because it was an acoustic show, the Four Voices tour was very much a "folk" presentation. And Chastity tours as essentially an acoustic duo with another guitar player. But neither of your records is tethered exclusively to folk. I've been thinking about "genre identity" lately and I feel like we should be letting artists self-identify. So how would each of you self-identify, if you had to?

ES: We need a word, with a musical application, that's like "queer."

CB: Yes!

ES: Until "queer" came along, there wasn't anything that didn't put us in a box.

KM: I feel like "Americana" is a little bit like "queer" because it can be specific, but it can also be an umbrella term.

CB: I love Americana. I feel completely like my heart is in Americana, but I don't always feel like I'm in the heart of Americana. So many of the [musicians] I love are still white men. I'm still an up-and-comer. I'm in such a different place than Emily, in that regard. But, in my mind, I'm an Americana-soul queer artist.

I love the idea of "queer." ... More and more, I love the sound of the word, linguistically, more than "lesbian." "Lesbian" just doesn't sound as good.

KM: I concur. "Queer" can also cover gender identity, orientation, etc. It's sort of a one-stop umbrella term, to me. That's why I use it, because it hits on all of my needs. What say you, Saliers?

ES: I go back and forth on this. Everybody needs a way to describe things. We just need that, linguistically. So we say "folk-rock" or whatever it is. Even I find myself asking, "What kind of music is it?" Since there's no word like "queer," we say "folk-rock-punk-R&B with a little bit of country" or something like that. And it just takes too long to say.

Sometimes it doesn't bother me. But there are times, it's like, "What's in a name?" [The answer is,] "A lot."

When I did my PledgeMusic campaign to finance my solo record, I said, "I don't want to be 'folk.' I don't want to be in the folk category." I had all this internal struggle with what it meant — like you were saying, Chastity, to be a queer woman with an acoustic guitar. ... I know how society looks at queer women with acoustic guitars. To me, that is the same thing as self-homophobia, which I've had to work through [for] years and years — not belonging, feeling the weight of society's judgment and what that meant. And I think [the fact that I have] any kind of hateful feelings toward [people] describing me as "folk" is like self-homophobia because of all the associations that go along with that.

But the other truth, my musical reality, [is that] it's not really folk music that moves me as much as it is black, Southern gospel or Chaka Khan or Mary J. Blige.

KM: Or Kendrick Lamar.

ES: Or Kendrick Lamar. Oh, my God. Brilliant, brilliant, brilliant record. But I don't write music like that. I'm not about to try to co-opt anything that deep and that associated with the realities of the people's lives who have created that music. So I just have to be stuck in a guitar player's body, a folk body — a folk shell. Internally, I'm a lot more than that and I'm moved by a lot more than that. ■

THE GLORY HOTEL

NEWLY RENOVATED ROOMS

RENTED MONTHLY

CLEAN   QUIET

SECURE

→

ATTENTION: VISITORS

FOR SECURITY PURPOSES, VISITORS MAY ONLY ENTER THE BUILDING WHEN ACCOMPANIED BY THE TENANT.

MANAGEMENT

AUTEUR RESEARCH

LEARNING TO LOVE YOURSELF

Leeroy Stagger leaves booze and fear behind to move his music forward

by David McPherson

AFTER TOILING IN THE margins of the roots music world for nearly two decades, releasing 10 critically acclaimed records, singer-songwriter Leeroy Stagger is ready for a bigger stage. His songs have been heard on hit television shows like *Grey's Anatomy, Sons of Anarchy, Degrassi,* and *Heartland*. His seventh album, *Radiant Land*, was nominated for Roots Solo Recording of the Year at the 2013 Western Canadian Music Awards. Despite all this, he remains relatively unknown.

Still, among his many fans is Los Lobos multi-instrumentalist Steve Berlin, who produced Stagger's 2015 release, *Dream It All Away*. "Leeroy Stagger is an extraordinarily talented singer, songwriter, and player," Berlin says. "He has a unique combination of street smarts and a comprehensive worldview that is rare among the current crop of young artists. ... I'm looking forward to what he does next."

What Stagger is doing next is baring his heart in his songwriting, giving his listeners something to feel good about in these troubled times, even as he occasionally comments on the world. Indeed, it's often challenging for a certain kind of songwriter to *not* offer an opinion. Political songwriting has been helpful for past generations, but most modern writers who approach that part of their craft have to grapple with the question of

how to share their views in a way that is helpful, not preachy. Yet, for 34-year-old Stagger, speaking up has always come naturally. He has a rare talent for penning topical songs that address social concerns against a backdrop of rocking out.

With his latest album *Love Versus* (released last spring), Stagger allows his optimism and hope to prevail alongside his topical tunes. He's feeling grateful for life and lets it show. "There are so many people out there suffering," he says. "I would rather try and make them feel better about themselves, at the very least. ... [That] begins with learning to love yourself. ... It's about loving the person you are, warts and all."

Love Versus is the first effort Stagger has recorded at his home studio in Southern Alberta and his first release with True North Records. For it, Stagger teamed up with producer Colin Stewart (Dan Mangan, Black Mountain), who pulled together a dream band for the project. The cornerstone was Pete Thomas, longtime drummer for Elvis Costello, who came up to Alberta from L.A. for the sessions, joining guitarist Paul Rigby (Neko Case), keyboardist Geoff Hilhorst (The Deep Dark Woods), and Stagger's longtime bassist Tyson Maiko. Over the course of three weeks, the group christened Stagger's new studio and changed his perspective on his art.

Stagger admits he didn't know what the record was going to sound like before

building the studio. He only knew that, after recording most of his records in a basement studio, he wanted a recording facility with high ceilings. "I also wanted [the studio] to be wood, like the gatefold of [Neil Young's] *Harvest*, without the big gaps in the boards because that wouldn't work too well in Alberta," he explains. "That's what I ended up with — this big, beautiful wood building that sounds and looks amazing. I didn't play a note of music in there until Pete Thomas showed up and started setting up his drums, because I was so exhausted [from building]. ... As soon as Pete started playing the drums, [Colin Stewart] and I looked at each other and shared smiles because we knew that the room sounded so good."

Stagger is the first to admit that his choice of Stewart, who typically works with loud rock bands, for this record was a little out of left field. But, he adds, "I wanted someone in that world just to give the record some youthfulness. He was pretty respectful to the material in a lot of ways. I think I could have been pushed even more outside my comfort zone, but I'm really happy with the results.

"I'm still fairly young," he adds. "I can save my folk records for my 40s."

Sober Thoughts

Like many artists before him, Stagger choose to pursue a career that was not the

> **"Even in this day and age, when there is a lot of emphasis on self care, there are still a lot of those among us who can't get out of a rut."**
>
> Leeroy Stagger

ideal one for an alcoholic. In his early years, he struggled with the drinking but has since confronted his demons and put his party lifestyle behind him.

Abused as a child, Stagger says he woke up one day and realized that he had to forgive himself for his past transgressions and forgive the people that were a part of his childhood in order to move on with his life. "I had to put all that to rest," he says. "For me, that's what my drinking was all about. ... I was just covering that up and self-medicating for longer than I was aware [I was doing that]. Finally, I just hit a wall."

It's been almost 10 years since his last drink, and Stagger says his sobriety is a key to his happiness, his spiritual outlook on life, and the work-life balance he has from day to day.

"It took me about seven years to even try a sip of a non-alcoholic beer because I was terrified. It's almost been 10 years now for me. Sure, it [drinking] crosses my mind. That's all part of it, but you get to a point where you say, 'Look at my life now versus then.' I've thought about drinking again and my sponsor told me, 'You could, but look at what you have in your life right now: a beautiful studio, two wonderful kids who have never seen you hungover or drunk, and your marriage is back on track. Do you really want to jeopardize all that?'" Instead, Stagger meditates to mellow his mind and sticks to what he does best: writing story-songs.

"I just got so exhausted of living like that," he says. "I was exhausted of being fearful of life and I hit a crossroads where I knew [either I had to] quit music and do something else, and see if I could find some joy in that, or continue on my music path. I met some pretty key people in my life that influenced me and inspired me to go look within myself and see if I could face my fears, and it worked — it's working. I think that's a lot of what this record is about.

"My kids are four and one right now," he adds. "A big part of my mental and spiritual outlook is to be able to function as a dad, and a dad that is gone a lot. I want to be there for my kids." Being there, he says, is about finding the right balance in his life as a touring musician, a husband, and a dad — something that he didn't see many examples of during his own formative years.

What's Precious

These days, gratitude runs deep in Stagger's life. It's not surprising, then, that it weaves its way into his most recent songs.

Take the title cut from *Love Versus*, which is a meditation on being present. "I didn't know what that track was really about until recently," he reflects. "It's a real nod to the human condition ... the struggle right now, especially of oppressed people. Someone the other day was mentioning

the Palestinian conflict to me and told me this big long story; then, later that night when I was singing that song I felt it really reflected that story I was told earlier in the day, with the lyrics I wrote like these: 'Try to feed our friends / put a bullet in our back / try to build a home to house us and you tear it down again.' I don't remember what the context was when I wrote that song, but it can really mean anything."

Another standout on *Love Versus* is "$1,500 a Day (Song for Elliott)." As someone who battled demons for a long time, Stagger saw something in Elliott Smith's tortured tale he felt he needed to explore in a song.

"I watched that documentary [*Heaven Adores You*] on Netflix," he says, "and there was something mentioned in the movie that at one point he was spending $1,500 a day on his drug habit, and that really jumped out at me. I had my party years, but they weren't $1,500 a day worth! That really struck a chord: This whole idea of success and fame ... a lot of times, artists are chasing [that], and a lot of times that's not the best thing for us. I just wish someone like Elliott could have dealt with his demons better and we all would have benefited. Even in this day and age, when there is a lot of emphasis on self care, there are still a lot of those among us who can't get out of a rut."

One of the most personal songs on *Love Versus* is "Little Brother." Stagger admits it's a "big song" about sibling love.

It reflects on the brevity of our time on this earth, and again the theme of gratitude seeps in as he tells the story of how his younger brother nearly died two years ago when he was in the back of a taxi that smashed into a telephone pole going 70 km/hr (around 45 mph) in a 40 km/hr (25 mph) zone. He wound up in a coma for three weeks and now, nearly a year and a half later, he's still recovering, though he has been helping with the merch table at Stagger's shows lately.

"That was intense, ... a big eye-opener for me," Stagger recalls. "Maybe it was also a bit of a catalyst for me to find some joy in my life, as opposed to the fear I was constantly living with. I realized that life is pretty precious. We are not here forever so I might as well try to have some fun along the way.

"It's kind of a bastion on this record — a very strong song with interesting production, something I've never done before," he continues. "I'm really proud of that song, and my brother loves it too. It's an emotional song for both of us. I explain the story during my shows and I always look over to him ... and he's got some tears in his eyes and people immediately flock to him and give him hugs. It's a special thing and he brings a lot of spirit to the band."

New Sounds

Stagger's family has been a big part of his music career, but his songwriting heroes are from the wider world, including Josh Rouse, Neil Young, Leonard Cohen, Tom Petty, Kathleen Edwards, and Steve Earle.

Stagger sports a tattoo on his right forearm that reads "El Corazón" in reference to one of Earle's best records. "He's definitely a big influence for me," says Stagger. "There are so many, though. Steve was a big influence until I was able to find my own voice. I probably imitated him a little too much in my early years and on my first few records. Having his seal of approval was the first step for me to move away from that and realize that I do have my own voice and that my songwriting is strong enough to stand on its own.

"I did some shows with him [Earle] years ago and his manager was putting out my records for a while," he adds. "It was an amazing experience. I'm so grateful, but I realized I don't need to be Steve Earle; he has his own pile of shit to deal with. My records started getting really good after that.

"I feel like I've been hitting my stride over the past three records," he adds, "but this one especially feels like I've set a new standard, and everything I do now has to live up to it."

Indeed, *Truth Be Sold* (2013) and *Dream It All Away* (2015) showed considerable growth, and *Love Versus* moves the songwriter's needle — and his comfort zone — even further into yet undiscovered musical territory by adding new sonic layers and creative instrumentations that stray just a wee bit farther from the roots-rock sounds that have characterized Stagger's songs to date while still keeping the hooks for which he's known. "I'm always a stickler for a hook and a melody," he says. "I love [Josh Ritter's and Josh Rouse's] turns of phrase,

their melodies, and their pop sensibilities."

"That's one thing that is cool about Leeroy," says guitarist Paul Rigby, who played on *Love Versus.* "He is really good at taking stock at where he is in his career, but at the same time always feeling like he can do other stuff. ... I feel this record is a step in the right direction for Leeroy to be Leeroy, and I don't think he's done yet. He is still a singer-songwriter, but he is not afraid of experimenting with new sounds." ∎

DAVID GUENTHER

TWO HEADS ARE BETTER THAN ONE

Talking with the Avett Brothers about simplicity, trust, and collaboration

by Kim Ruehl

ONE BALMY NIGHT THIS PAST summer in Golden, Colorado, Scott and Seth Avett took the stage at the Red Rocks Amphitheater to play their songs for a sold-out crowd. It was a big gig for a pair of brothers from the small town of Mount Pleasant, North Carolina, who came up making music with their family. Having written and sung their way up the musical totem pole since their 2002 debut, on this final night in a three-show run, they had clearly become comfortable with the space — the way this beautiful, natural amphitheater seemingly opens the music right up to the sky.

As the brothers and their sizable backing band (Bob Crawford on bass, Joe Kwon on cello, Tania Elizabeth on violin, Paul Defiglia on keys, and Mike Marsh on drums) pounced from song to song, pulling from across their vast catalog, the packed crowd sang every word, throwing their heads back and raising their arms up. Indeed, one thing that has carried across the Avett Brothers' nine studio albums in 15 years is songs with accessible melodies and easy-flowing lyricism — the kind of songs that beg to be sung along with.

They opened this night with "Shame" from their 2007 release *Emotionalism*, with its drinking song-like chorus and everyone's-been-there lyrics:

Okay, so I was wrong about
My reasons for us falling out
of love. I want to fall back in.
My life is different now, I swear
I know now what it means to care
About somebody other than myself.

But where any songwriter can lay down a stream-of-consciousness confession, a wish that they hadn't broken off a meaningful relationship, the magic comes in lines that instinctively carry the singer along, like a gust of wind under a falling leaf. These lines in "Shame" are breezy, with an AAB/CCD rhyme scheme in iambic tetrameter — a poetic rhythm measured by four pairs of syllables, with the emphasis on every other syllable. Each third line hops away to let the music take the lead and keep the listener guessing.

"Shame" isn't the only song that does this, of course. "Once and Future Carpenter" from their 2012 release, *The Carpenter,* similarly alternates emphasis, like a horse on a dirt road, clomping along, occasionally stumbling over a rock or root but persisting nonetheless:

Forever I will move
Like the world that turns beneath me
When I lose my direction,
I'll look up to the sky
And when the black cloak
drags along the ground
I'll be ready to surrender,
and remember
We're all in this together.

That last line brings up the other threads that run through all of the Avett

"You've got to write bad songs. You've got to write a lot more of those than the good ones. You've got to be resolved to the idea that they're not all going to get shared in your lifetime."

Scott Avett

Brothers' songwriting: persistence, hope, trust — and, notably, collaboration. These are not just threads that *happen* to pop up in their songs; they are the very foundation upon which the pair's music-making was built. As brothers, they have built their career on a bond of trust and collaboration that has driven them through personal tribulations the way only the love of a family can.

When I got a moment to talk with them during MerleFest earlier this year, we started with the concept of collaboration. Our interview has been edited for length and clarity.

KIM RUEHL: Collaboration always scared me in my songwriting years, because you have to give something up. If you're the kind of songwriter who's just writing personal stuff, when you bring it to someone else their stuff comes in and changes what you're saying.

SETH AVETT: I think one of the driving components to there being a fear to collaboration is that your idea might get taken advantage of or you might get taken advantage of. Scott and I don't have that concern because we're brothers. We know that we're going to treat the other's efforts with the utmost respect and we've proven as much over

the years. It's never been an issue, as far as having a fear about sharing something. To work on something on your own is just a natural act if you're an artist.

KR: Yeah. I would imagine that, especially being brothers, you can pull things out of each other that you'd be afraid to get to on your own, or that maybe you wouldn't know were there if you weren't writing with someone who knows you so well.

SETH: It tempers our ideas a lot. [If] one of us started something, whatever the other one brings — another part or another layer — makes it a much more interesting piece. That moment in the song where another person starts singing and it feels refreshing, we have that kind of built in all the time.

SCOTT AVETT: This applies to when we worked with [producer] Rick Rubin as well. Two or three heads are better than one, you know? [That gives us a] better take on what a community of people [might] hear and think about. A lot of times, one of us on our own will completely miss the fact that what we just said is offensive. Or we'll completely miss the fact that what we said was really not quite what we were trying to say, but we'll find that out from each other. It's like

[having] a mediator in a way, which is what Rick did with us. He was the guy who settles the indecision or disagreement. Bob [Crawford does] that as well. He was the original mediator for us — not that we have big conflicts, but sometimes we don't see the same thing or can't really understand, and someone else can say something that can help us.

It feels really good to be taken advantage of sometimes. It feels really good to just let go ... throw away [your hangups and inhibitions]. Especially with family. If you have children, you've got to throw it all away, every bit of it. That's when life really starts happening. With us, the way our band has grown, it demands a lot of [letting go]. Having a wonderful, big life with a partner and having to give up in a way when you have children, and that sacrifice, you get to be repaid by playing with a great band.

KR: What about the songs you don't use? I know sometimes it feels really good to write a song, but that doesn't mean it's actually a *good* song. I guess that goes back to the idea of letting go.

SCOTT: You've got to write bad songs. You've got to write a lot more of those than the good ones. You've got to be resolved to the idea that they're not all going to get shared in your lifetime or you won't be

there to be part of the sharing.

We write a lot of songs that don't see the light of day in the construct of a band putting out a record. I mean, [being] a band putting out a record, for us, is 10-12 songs every two years. That's a very limited view of what we're thinking about and what [kind of music] we're trying to make. So we definitely have to wrap our heads around the idea that very little of this is going to be part of the community we have with our audience.

KR: You moved to New York for a while ...

SETH: I did, for about a year.

SCOTT: Seth did briefly, but we've never really ... abandoned our homes in North Carolina. That hasn't been our master plan; it wasn't designed like that, it's just been [that] each little step called for us to stay.

Especially as my family grows, I really see the value in a small life and the value of maintaining. What I mean by a small life is one where I don't get my mind blown daily. [I'm] trying really hard to be content with less.

I can't even imagine what would happen to my work schedule if I lived in New York or Nashville or Los Angeles, because I couldn't say no. I have this ambition that would allow me to go write or play with [someone like] John Prine, if I lived in Nashville and he was living there. You know, that's an example of the many things that [I would jump at] if I was lucky enough to have an opportunity. But [we've stayed here] out of love of place and region and the seasons and the natural world that is North Carolina. ...

We have so many thoughts and ideas. We've been getting together at home studios in our own space, to find out what happens to work at home instead of Malibu or New York. The calmness, the

tone that comes out of the calmness ... we were just talking on the bus about logistics, and what I've found, logistically, about staying in a small town in North Carolina, things are slower. Records are going to come out slower, everything is slower. That'll show, that'll transfer. It's probably a good thing, a good limitation.

KR: What's your favorite song to play?

SETH: I really like "Blackberry Blossom." At this moment, that's one of my favorite songs. It's one of those cyclical fiddle tunes that ... if you get in the groove of it you could probably play it for 15 or 20 minutes and be fine, which is a rarity for me. It feels like waking up in the morning and starting your day. It makes me feel all right.

SCOTT: When this band started, Seth and I were involved with another group of guys and it was a rock band, and at some point it all simplified into just us. It seemed so obvious but it took a while to get to, it took a lot of pain to get to. I think about songs and fiddle tunes, [and the simplicity of them] is always looming over Coachella and the Grammys. These simple tunes are over all of music. Just like the color wheel is sitting at the top of all great paintings. You look up at this seemingly simple thing that is really the answer and the puzzle piece to it all. These fiddle tunes, you go back to them and you play them, [and] it's like John Hartford said, something akin to, "Fifteen minutes in is when you really find the heart of these songs." Playing that AABB over and over and over. We experience something when we play these tunes.

KR: It's like a meditation.

SETH: Right, and there is a[n element of] letting it be about these songs. The melodies are wonderful, it's all natural. I guess they can technically be considered

"good songs," but there's nothing needed. You don't need an exciting sound or a beat or whatever. As they are, [they're] simple.

The lyrics push you to think about a certain thing. The melodies were very much like the seasons [in that] they take their time. They're not about virtuosity or great dynamics. They somehow mirror life in a way that's very centered.

KR: So with all that in mind, where do you go from *True Sadness*? You kind of cracked into the core of why people make music with that one — we're always reaching for each other. How can you go any deeper than that?

SCOTT: Maybe we don't. Maybe we're

needing to go shallow. Maybe we've been needing to do that for years. Every time we put a record out, we go, "Let's not make one that's so brooding, let's stay away from death on this one." But we really can't.

SETH: Scott and I both have this great desire to respect tradition, and I was looking at our set list and I got to "Vanity" and "Country Blues" and I just laughed at myself. Like, we can't help it. We cannot help it. We *can't* help it. In our minds, we're on this side of the fence, but then we get on the stage and we just cannot help but present some sort of rock and roll thing that's a little bent for the environment.

SCOTT: But Doc [Watson] did that too. He did everything. He took it and ... Dad was talking about the songs that Doc would do, and I said, 'Doc would do any song.' If he liked it, he would do it. If you start digging, you'd hear him do songs from all over the planet. That's an example to be taken from, not just the way we see them, like this [artist is] country or this one's old-time. They were interpreters. You don't look at John Coltrane and say he played the sax well and played jazz well. We revere him because he interpreted and tapped into something that was inside of him.

SETH: Right, like there's some right way

to [write songs] or some wrong way. The audience we play for and the things that eventually come back to us, that's really where the dialogue is about what's right and what's wrong. ...

That simplicity is great to get back to. We've reset a lot in our career.

Our career — we've never thought of it as our career. This is our life. We're always going to make music no matter what happens in our lives, but simplicity is a place we're always going to reset to. That's something that Rick Rubin has helped us with — we need to hear those lyrics. We need to make some space and simplify. ∎

INNER CHILD

After rock stardom with the Presidents of the United States of America, Chris Ballew found his voice in music for kids

by Corbie Hill

> **"I spend a lot of time in an imaginary space: a car with a family of five in it, leaving Yosemite National Park after a long day of hiking in the summer, in a five-hour traffic jam. They all have to pee, they're all hungry, they're all mad at each other, the kids are crying. You put the CD in, and it should help."**
> Chris Ballew

CHRIS BALLEW IS WATCHING a tree come down. "What the heck are they doing?" he says, craning his neck to get a better view. The tree used to have a companion, which was felled months ago. Now a crew is sawing away at this one. Over the course of an hour they dismantle it, piece by piece. At 52 years old, Ballew knows the grown-up facts: The tree is not on his land, and he has no say in whether it lives or dies. Yet there's something in the way he watches it come down, some form of existential longing so deep, so pure, you'd swear he was a second-grader losing his favorite climbing tree.

Ballew lives on Vashon Island, west of Seattle in Puget Sound, among undeveloped valleys, and he has intentionally let the grass grow wild. This has created a prime habitat for bugs, snakes, and birds — the animals whose unknowable inner lives have fascinated Ballew since he was a child. Here, away from the chaos, noise, and distraction of grown-up rock and roll and heavy touring, Ballew has returned to his natural state.

Years ago, he was the singer and principal songwriter of the Presidents of the United States of America, his "grown-up band," whose 1995 self-titled debut went multiplatinum on the strength of singles like "Peaches" and "Lump." Nowadays, Ballew records and performs under the name Caspar Babypants, making innocent, quirky children's music at an impressive clip. He released *Jump For Joy!*, his 13th album in nine years, in August, and Ballew has already nearly wrapped up work on his next two albums. Between song fragments and traditional numbers he hasn't recorded yet, he thinks he could easily make it to 20. Despite his international radio hits, now that he's found his way to writing songs for families, Ballew feels at peace. "I was supposed to be Caspar Babypants my entire life," he says, "but I didn't know it."

Each one of the hundreds of songs on his Caspar Babypants records has gone through the same rigorous process: Working mostly alone, Ballew writes and rewrites each tune until it feels ready. Alongside the originals, he carefully arranges — and sometimes reimagines — traditional songs and nursery rhymes. Once in his studio, Ballew records layers of instruments and harmonies. Then he puts the song aside for six-or-so months, granting himself as much distance as possible before he begins his editing process, which he refers to as the "mute party." This requires a bit of ruthlessness, as he listens to the recording and eliminates any extraneous sounds or lines. He says he can't let his ego get in the way, because a keyboard part he worked hard on and was once proud of may not have a place in the final track. Like a sculptor knocking away huge chunks of sound, Ballew mutes and mutes — there goes the banjo, there goes the mandolin, maybe the drums — until he's found the core of the song.

"I spend a lot of time in an imaginary space," he says. "[It's] a car with a family of five in it, leaving Yosemite National Park after a long day of hiking in the summer, in a five-hour traffic jam. They all have to pee, they're all hungry, they're all mad at each other, the kids are crying. You put the CD in, and it should help."

Into Inner Lives

Ballew grew up on a cul-de-sac on the edge of Seattle's suburbs. He's always been close with his brother Tim, who's 20 months younger. Next door was Dave Thiele, and the three formed the nucleus of a close-knit playgroup.

"[Chris] has known me since I was born and he's friends with my older brother," Thiele says. "I was best man at his wedding, he was best man at my wedding. That kind of thing."

From the start, imagination was key to their friendships. When Chris and Tim were very young, for instance, they would lose themselves in games of make-believe, creating little worlds together down by the baseboards. They developed personalities and hierarchies for their stuffed animals, for whom they'd build little houses. Even as a kid, Tim says, Chris was fascinated by the inner lives of inanimate objects, bugs, and woodland creatures.

When they were still in elementary school, Chris and Thiele formed a band. "We were called David and the Overtones and we had one song, called 'David and the Overtones,'" Thiele says. He chuckles at the cuteness of two little kids forming a rock band in a suburban basement, but points out that Ballew was already taking piano lessons and really applying himself.

As time passed, Ballew honed these skills further, dedicating the same imagination and attention to detail to making music as he had to creating worlds with his stuffed animals. "[Chris] lived further out in the suburbs growing up than I did, and I think he was always a little bit of a different kind of dude," says Dave Dederer, who played three-string "guitbass" in Presidents before leaving the band in 2004. "Especially once he got a cassette four-track sometime in high school, spending time making music was just as exciting and rewarding as anything else."

As a teenager, Ballew took on odd jobs that gave him the space to allow his mind to trail off into his own world. One of his favorites was at the Fun Forest, a rundown amusement park that used to be near Seattle's Space Needle. Thiele, who also worked there, recalls that it was a crappy job. The hours were long, and all they had to do was hang out by a ride and press the start or stop button, and occasionally hose out puke. Yet Ballew's hard work there paid off when he scored the coveted job of operating the roller coaster.

"Even though it paid really low and it was long [hours] and most people would find it really, really boring," says Thiele, "I think he liked that he could just go someplace and get paid to think about songs and music, and just live in his imagination."

After graduating high school in 1983, Ballew headed east, attending State University of New York at Purchase and then moving to Boston. It was there that he first encountered "Spider" John Koerner. Ballew had written songs about animals for years, but he'd always thought of them as second-class citizens, he says. Then he wandered into a Boston bar to find Koerner playing to a near-empty room.

"Turns out he's a legendary dude as far as the '60s folk and blues scene in Manhattan goes," Ballew says. "He had ended up in Boston, [and] he ended up playing for nobody on this Thursday afternoon in a bar.

"The music blew me away, because it was this old folk music, but it was about chickens and frogs and monkeys," he adds. "It had the weight and history behind it in the vibe, but it also had these whimsical themes, and that's when I realized, 'I can write songs about animals and not think of them as less-than.'" In 2011, Ballew paid tribute to the folk legend when he wrote the song "Spider

John" for his *Sing Along!* album.

Innocence and Innuendo

In the early '90s, Ballew returned to Seattle and soon began playing once again with Thiele and their friend Dederer. In the fall of 1993, Ballew and Dederer formed the Presidents of the United States of America with drummer Jason Finn. (Though Thiele wasn't in the Presidents, he's a sort of "fifth Beatle" who played in a number of bands leading up to it.) The core of the Presidents, and one reason the group's eponymous debut sold so well and spawned a number of

radio hits, is that the trio's work balanced innocence with innuendo. "Peaches," for instance, isn't really about fruit.

"At the time, I had just recently been through a dark period in life, lots of tortured love experiences and relationships," Chris says. "So some sort of grown-up themes started to sprinkle into my burgeoning innocent songwriting." The combination resonated beautifully with audiences in the Pacific Northwest. The Presidents' uninhibited live show didn't hurt, either.

"Grunge had kind of taken hold by then, and people [in Seattle] were so responsive to the Presidents," Ballew's brother Tim recalls. The scene was dominated by brooding, self-serious hard rock acts, he adds, who adopted a "fuck you for coming" attitude and stared at their shoes onstage. That wasn't Chris, though — Chris had fun.

"The Presidents were amazing for this kind of joyful audience engagement," Tim says. "I was struck by the electricity in the room." Yet Tim recognized something deeply familiar in this raucous, sometimes silly rock band. "All these Presidents songs, if you sift through them, [Chris] was writing about bugs, he was writing about the inner life of things. He was still that same kid that was playing with stuffed animals and imagining these elaborate inner perspectives. It was just clothed in the rock clothes."

Over time, Ballew kept the innocence in his songwriting and let the innuendo fall away. His life had changed — he was in a major rock band, selling albums and touring like crazy, and he worked through the things that had been bothering him. Now, Ballew thinks this is why the Presidents' first album resonated and the other ones didn't. He didn't have that kind of sadness to write about anymore, so the innocence-and-innuendo equation just wasn't available.

But even in the mid-'90s there were hints of the musician Ballew would later become. When the Presidents signed with Columbia Records, for instance, he suggested to his bandmates that they stop touring, and instead just play five nights a week in Seattle. Fans could come see the animals in their natural habitat, he suggested.

"At that time, we were sandwiched in between Janet Jackson and Madonna on MTV," he says. "The idea got shot down immediately and we went on traditional tours, but I didn't like it."

Ballew enjoys traveling, but not touring. He finds the road life boring and exhausting, and it wears on his nervous system. He notes that it's hard to eat healthy on tour, and missing home is a drag. Even if you're staying at the Four Seasons, as Dederer notes, you can't make a peanut butter and jelly sandwich with peanut butter, jelly, and bread from your own kitchen if you wake up hungry in the middle of the night. Ultimately, touring was a poor fit for Ballew, and, as time went on, so was playing with a band.

In his teenage years, and then in his early 20s in Boston, Ballew had developed an almost monastic approach to creating music. He holed up in whatever crappy little apartment he was

living in at the time, subsisting on beans and losing himself in four-track recording projects.

"I'm way more in service to the songs than [I am] interested in the group experience of being in a band," Ballew says, adding that he needs to be in a space where he can listen to a recording, hear that the bass and guitar need to go, and have the freedom to drop those instruments from the track. He needs to be in the position to mute every instrument but a ukulele or a keyboard, for example, if that's what sounds best in the end. "If you're in a band, that's hard to describe to the other band members and have them feel okay about [you] saying, 'I don't want any drums on this entire album,'" he says. "The drummer's going to be sad about that."

As a member of the Presidents, Ballew didn't get that kind of agency, and it stressed him out to the point that he was having panic attacks. It was unsustainable — he's since quit the band twice. He formed several other bands, including one with rappers Sir Mix-a-Lot (who revolutionized Ballew's process by introducing him to recording with computers) and Mike "Outtasite" Singleton (who later contributed to the Caspar Babypants version of "Them

> ## "Being joyful and silly is my favorite way to be. To me, that feels like a more honest expression of having arrived at a place of enlightenment than any other form of expression."
>
> Chris Ballew

Bones"). But nothing stuck until 2008, when Ballew started work on Caspar Babypants' debut album. He was finally able to look back at his time in the Presidents calmly and dispassionately. That band was like a worn-out old suit that had fit in his youth, he says, but not anymore. It was time to take it to Goodwill.

"The Presidents," he says, "are [part of] a long line of breadcrumbs that I left for myself, my whole life, that were leading me toward my ultimate destination, which is Caspar Babypants and music for families."

A Secret Gear

As Caspar Babypants, Ballew has creative and practical control. He's the artist, the label, and the distribution service. He does his own bookings and simply doesn't tour; if you want to see a Caspar Babypants show, you must travel to the Pacific Northwest. He plays a hundred-plus shows a year, all in the middle of the day and all within 90 minutes of his house. He likes this setup because he can drop his daughter off at high school, go play a show at a library, and be done in time to pick her up.

"He's had all sorts of offers to make it bigger, to get a national booking agent," says Dederer. "[But he knows] what he wants and [is] disciplined about it."

Ballew has also learned that he needs time and space to recharge. He's always been intuitively drawn to meditation without even knowing that's what he was doing or that he needed to create that time and space for himself. He just thought he was listening to Brian Eno and staring at nothing — he didn't realize that was meditative and essential to his mental health.

"I think part of why I felt sad and weird in a rock band was I didn't realize how much downtime I need and how much quiet time I need," he says. He explains the human psyche in terms of a car's gearbox. You can be in a high gear, zooming around, getting stuff done, or you can access a lower gear and slow down. Ballew describes meditation as finding another, almost secret gear, one that's absolute dead stop. You lose your body, and your identity, he says, and touch the fabric of the universe, simply by stopping so totally. He goes into this space three or four times a day. It's how he recharges, how he zeroes in on his best self. "Being joyful and silly is my favorite way to be," he says. "To me, that feels like a more honest expression of having arrived at a place of enlightenment than any other form of expression."

There's plenty of silly in his oeuvre, too, in songs like "Stompy the Bear," "Free Couch," "My Pants are on Vacation," "Chicken in the Cornbread," and dozens upon dozens more, but that's not Ballew's only speed. Like any songwriter, he processes his life through music.

In "Baby and the Animals" and his version of "Pop Goes the Weasel," Ballew sings metaphorically about his own experiences in the music industry. There are wistful tunes like "Tumble," "Sun Go," or "Baby Cloud," and spooky ones like "Mysterious Things" and "Woods Behind My Home." In the latter, he draws on both his edge-of-the-suburbs childhood and his lifelong fascination with little creatures' inner lives.

There's a million crickets playing violins, sounding like a symphony
They'll do their best if I request a certain melody
The concert hall is extremely small, but what a happy tone
We hatch a plan to form a band in the woods behind my home.

Yet, as Caspar Babypants, Ballew also sings about un-silly things like death. He wrote "Dragonfly Blue," for instance, after losing a close friend. In the chorus of this gently melancholic song, he simply pleads, "Please don't go away, don't go away, don't go away."

"So yeah," he quips. "I process complex emotions on these albums, too."

Ballew's ability to wield as broad an emotional palette in children's music as one might in "adult" music is one reason Caspar Babypants resonates. There's just nothing patronizing here. Many children's musicians take a gee-golly, "Hey, kids!" approach, and proceed to either give kids instructions or try to pass for a happy, fun adult. It's almost a transactional relationship, Ballew's brother Tim points out, which kids see through. Caspar Babypants, meanwhile, is simply Ballew being his regular, unguarded self.

"That feeling was always there," Tim says. "When he transitioned to the Caspar Babypants stuff … it was almost like removing the artifice from it. It was more naturally his voice."

Nobody understands this better than Ballew, who has finally found his truest songwriting voice through writing for children like the one he used to be. "I'm not writing things I think kids will like," he explains. "I'm writing what I like as an adult who nurtures childlike perspective all day. I don't want to be a grownup who hangs out with children; I want to be a child!" ∎

The Way It Goes

by David Olney

All touring songwriters need a strategy for staying awake on those endless, all-night drives that always seem to come after the last gig of a tour. Some folks chug coffee, but I like to keep alert by going over the lyrics of Townes Van Zandt's "Pancho and Lefty" — line by line, word by word. It's such a visual song, so cinematic. Each verse and chorus calls up distinct pictures, which, in turn, trigger my own personal memories and images. Its cryptic storyline could carry a number of different scenarios, which makes it a good mental exercise as the white lines tick by on the highway. Often, I'll have knocked out 200 miles without hardly noticing by the time I get to the last line of this masterpiece.

In case you have any long drives coming up, I thought I'd share some analysis to get you thinking. Here's an abbreviated version of my thought process:

Living on the road, my friend
Was bound to make you free
and clean ...

Who is being addressed here? A road musician? Maybe. An outlaw? Likely. Maybe both. We have to wait to answer that question.

Now you wear your skin like iron
And your breath's as hard as
kerosene.

So much for the romance of the road. The image is so stark and unflinching. There's no self-pity in these lines. Road life might bring a measure of freedom, but it will also desensitize you, make your skin like metal, and the omnipresent booze will make your breath like poison. Musician or outlaw, your soul gets some serious wear and tear.

You weren't your mama's only boy
But her favorite one, it seems
She began to cry when you said
goodbye
And sank into your dreams.

Here's the heartbreak of a mother watching her child go wrong. Not necessarily wrong in a legal sense but, more likely, wrong emotionally, when moodiness turns to isolation, when sadness descends to depression. Dreams should lift us up, but here they weigh a vulnerable person down.

Pancho was a bandit, boys
With a horse as fast as polished steel ...

Suddenly, the song switches to the third person. A gallant Mexican bandit is riding a high-spirited silver stallion. Immediately, we think of Pancho Villa, but also of Emiliano Zapata. In this one line, we know how this tale will end: the death of the noble hero. It will be sad but not surprising, and our expectations will be satisfactorily fulfilled.

He wore his gun outside his pants
For all the honest world to feel.

This is one of the great out-of-left-field lines I've ever heard. It takes such chances. Obviously, it could be taken as a sexual metaphor. But a metaphor for what? Somehow, it blasts past the phallic imagery.

Pancho wears a gun because he is an outlaw; he wears it outside his pants because he is unashamed of being outside the law. And if any honest soul cares to check out his gun, Pancho is okay with it and will not hide his true nature. Pancho is Pancho, and a gun is a gun.

Pancho met his match, you know,
On the desert down in Mexico.
No one heard his dying words
Ah, but that's the way it goes.

There is a story that Pancho Villa's last words were, "Don't let it end like this. Tell them I said something important." It's unlikely that Villa actually said this, but that's the nature of legend: You must take the true with the untrue. That's the way it goes.

All the Federales say
They could have had him any day.
They only let him hang around
Out of kindness, I suppose.

Here, the Mexican military arrives on the scene. They are a cross between a Greek chorus and the Keystone Cops. You can almost picture them in their snappy uniforms with their drooping mustaches. We listen to them lie that they outwitted Pancho, that they had the situation under control and only prolonged it to be magnanimous. We know them for the cowardly frauds they are.

Let's stop for a moment and look back on how far we have traveled: Two verses and a chorus. The first verse is a

sympathetic message to a hard-living friend with reference to his long-suffering mother. The second verse suddenly goes into a cinematic saga of a dashing Mexican bandit too good and honest to survive in a perfidious world. The chorus presents a troop of lying soldiers, too spineless to admit that Pancho was more than a match for them.

We're only getting started.

Lefty, he can't sing the blues
All night long like he used to ...

A new character enters: Lefty, the singer of blues.

The Latin word for "left" is *sinistra*, from which we also get "sinister." Already we have an insight into this man. He can't be trusted. He can't sing the blues anymore and he used to go all night long. Why?

The dust that Pancho bit down south
Ended up in Lefty's mouth.

I believe these two lines comprise the greatest lyric ever written. Biting the dust is a phrase that goes back to Homer's *Iliad*. Many a Greek and Trojan warrior has bitten the dust when they died before the walls of Troy. It's such a

strange and weirdly descriptive phrase. But to take the dust a warrior bites in death and transfer it to someone else's mouth is shockingly brilliant. With this couplet, we know at once that Lefty sold Pancho out to the Federales.

The day they laid poor Pancho low
Lefty split for Ohio.
Where he got the bread to go
There ain't nobody knows.

Well, the listener knows: The Federales paid Lefty just as the authorities paid Judas to betray Jesus. There is so much happening in this verse. To use the words "split" and "bread" moves the story out of myth into the modern world. "Split" and "bread" are hipster words. Here they signal a downward movement from the heroic to the cowardly. Besides, Ohio is about as far away from the exotic Mexican desert as you can get.

All the Federales say
They could have had him any day.
They only let him slip away
Out of kindness, I suppose.

The return of the Mexican-Greek chorus. There's a slight change in their

story here. The first time around, they only let Pancho hang around out of kindness.

This time, they only let him slip away out of kindness. It's a small change but it adds depth to the tale. It's as if the Federales can't quite keep their stories straight.

> *The poets tell how Pancho fell,*
> *Lefty's living in a cheap hotel.*
> *The desert's quiet and*
> *Cleveland's cold,*
> *So the story ends we're told.*

We glorify Pancho in poetry and song because we love our heroes and revile those who do them in. But Lefty is worse than a villain. He didn't kill Pancho in hand-to-hand combat. He killed him through treachery and deceit. His reward is a dismal, chilly room in the outskirts of hell, better known as Cleveland.

> *Pancho needs your prayers it's true,*
> *But save a few for Lefty, too.*
> *He just did what he had to do,*
> *And now he's growing old.*

Another unforeseen twist. Instead of damning Lefty, we are asked to pray for him. His fate is much worse than Pancho's. And without Lefty's treachery, Pancho's heroism would not be worthy of song. We've seen this played out countless times: Judas and Jesus, Iago and Othello, Robert Ford and Jesse James, Joe Frazier and Muhammad Ali. The saint needs a sinner and God needs the devil. Lefty was just doing what he had to do so that Pancho could be glorified. He had his role, and he played it well.

> *A few gray Federales say*
> *We could have had him any day,*
> *We only let him slip away*
> *Out of kindness, I suppose.*

For the last time, the Federales, now old and feeble and fewer in number, attempt to make their case that they had Pancho under control. Once again, a line has changed in their pathetic story. Well, let them go. Like Lefty, they're only doing what they have to do. That's the way it goes.

There are other ways to interpret this song, of course — hidden meanings and nuances I haven't touched on. But that's for another time. For now, long live Pancho. Long live Lefty. Long live Townes Van Zandt. ∎

CRACK YOU WIDE OPEN

Studying songwriting in New Mexico with Eliza Gilkyson, Gretchen Peters, and Mary Gauthier

by Kim Ruehl

THE TINY, WALKABLE TOWN of Arroyo Seco, New Mexico, stands around 7,600 feet above sea level, between the neighboring tourist haven of Taos and the near-11,000-foot Lucero Peak. The downtown area occupies the vertex of two county roads, and if you follow one of them north and turn left as it curves out of the village, it'll take you even higher, along the rim of a ridge, where Taos sits in a valley in the distance.

On that ridge, you'll find Casa de Musica, the part-time home of Texas-based singer-songwriter Eliza Gilkyson, who regularly welcomes strangers to her living room for songwriting retreats. She purchased the home four summers ago and has been fixing it up, bit by bit, ever since. She's revitalized the orchard in the backyard, fighting for water rights in this arid locale, and the trees look healthy and full of life, ringed with mulch and blossoming with fruit. For all her work on them, their presence feels effortless, much the same as her music. There are nooks and crannies around the home, both inside and out, tailor-made for sitting and thinking and writing a tune.

The woman from whom Gilkyson purchased the house was an old lesbian who had no legal connection to her partner when she died, so it took the family years to sort out who got to keep the house. In the meantime, it fell into disrepair and was taken over by a family of black bears — their claws left still-visible evidence of their occupation on the tree trunks and terra cotta tiles of the courtyard. The bears still visit some nights, when the plum tree bears its fruit.

The house's back door has a painting of a black bear hanging on it, like a welcome mat.

In Gilkyson's cozy living room last July, I joined her and her friends Mary Gauthier and Gretchen Peters and 21 students from around the country for a three-and-a-half-day songwriting retreat.

The gathering began on a Thursday evening, as students trickled into the house, past a dining room table stocked with pieces of flourless chocolate cake garnished with raspberries and cream. The hosts welcomed everyone to New Mexico, then got down to business. Gilkyson warned everyone about altitude sickness and apologized for accidentally buying one-ply toilet paper in preparation for the event, an admission that broke the ice for the roomful of nervous writers unsure of what they'd

Photos of Taos, New Mexico, by Brett Leigh Dicks

signed up for. Then, one by one, in a circle that spanned the room, each person introduced themselves and talked about what moved them to come.

A few of those folks make music for a living, from Austin, Los Angeles, New England, and they were hoping to brush up on their skills by rubbing elbows with some of their songwriting heroes. But most of the class was comprised of people who have dabbled through the years, some who just started making music recently, who have felt pulled toward songwriting and are looking for guidance

about where to start — teachers, counselors, retirees, and others for whom music is an escape or an entrée, depending.

The stories about how each of these people came to the music, how they decided to spend a thousand dollars (plus travel, lodging, food, transportation) on this retreat, were deeply moving, as was the openness with which Gauthier, Gilkyson, and Peters met them. The very little effort it took for a bubble to form around the room — a safe haven of open, creative sharing — was itself a reminder

of how connected all people are. That a song doesn't need to traverse a wide chasm; it only needs to be a thread. Observing this welcome circle, I could see eyes and hearts opening wider already, the unexpected and guarded awakening of strangers who have just begun to realize they are not alone.

Peters — a Nashville-based writer whose often gut-wrenching, deeply poetic songs have been recorded by artists as varied as Etta James, Shania Twain, and Neil Diamond — announced, "We're here to crack you wide open." It was an

ambitious, provocative statement, to be sure. But as the weekend unfolded and tears were shed (Gauthier had warned, "There will be tears, but I like to call them 'old tears'"), the novelty of this beautiful location, with its breathtaking view in the Land of Enchantment, fell away. All that mattered was the surface tension of the moment, the music that lowered each of these strangers to the depths of their selves, to find the right configuration of words, rhythm, and melody that would free them of whatever imagined distance exists between individuals. Songwriting,

after all, is about connection, about our common humanity.

Gilkyson, who has participated in several songwriting retreats, notes that this particular retreat "turned out to be the best workshop I've hosted there. So much information passed along and everyone had the most amazing breakthroughs by the last day. People pushed through a lot of doubts and constraints and really recommitted to the process.

"It's easy to write songs," she adds. "It's hard to write *good* songs, where something uniquely 'you' comes up from

the deep and makes its mark. It's fun to be a part of that excursion into the deep end."

On Friday morning, as a guitar was passed around the room for a sharing session, it became clear that a couple of people were grappling with the way religion has forced space between them and their families. Others were struggling with love and loss, pain and longing. One woman's wick had been lit by the story of her ancestors, who were orphaned in childhood on the Western frontier, and she wanted to delve into the exceptional sadness and fear they must have felt as

they determined to survive alone from such a young age. There was a power in their persistence that she wanted to tap for herself, and, as generations of humans have discovered, there was something in the telling of that story that could reveal to her how to take the next steps in her own life.

Songwriting, after all, can be a pathway to healing through empathy and understanding. It challenges us to distill the most impossible, enormous, fleeting emotions down to digestible amounts. Everyone has felt lonely, for example, but it was songwriter Hank Williams who

named it with the line, "I'm so lonesome I could cry." Everyone craves redemption, but it was songwriter Mary Gauthier who named it with the line, "Every single one of us could use a little mercy now." Everyone encounters the complexities of inner conflict, but songwriter Gretchen Peters simplified it with her line, "I loved the fighter and the bull."

Indeed it was that song, "The Matador," that Peters pulled out when the guitar landed on her and it became time for the three hosting songwriters to share their examples of exquisite writing. It wasn't an opportunity to show off so much as a way

to reconnect everyone in the room with each writer's individual voice, show without telling what it means to write a very good song, and perhaps convince those present that everyone has songs in them — you just have to find them.

"We don't want you to believe we've written the final song on any subject," Gilkyson impressed upon her students. "We believe that in you is the same capacity."

Mary's Little Speech

As beautiful and enchanting as

Gilkyson's New Mexico home is, the retreat these three songwriters throw there is not unusual. On other occasions, Gilkyson has teamed up with songwriters' songwriter John Gorka for a similar gathering in the same location. In New York state, Dar Williams holds an annual event called Writing a Song That Matters. Elsewhere in New York, Steve Earle holds Camp Copperhead. Ellis Paul throws the New England Songwriters Retreat each year in Connecticut, and Uncle Earl alum Kristin Andreassen joins with fiddler Laura Cortese to head the Miles of

Music Camp in New Hampshire. For those seeking a serious getaway, Shawn Colvin, Judy Collins, and Patty Griffin held a nine-day "salon" in Patmos, Greece, last summer titled "How the Light Gets In: Music, Memoir, and the Art of Telling Our Stories."

These are a smattering of events, but there have been numerous others in recent years, as full-time, celebrated singer-songwriters have found that teaching is a way to ensure a reliable paycheck in a constantly changing music industry that also lets them dig deeper into their own relationship with

their craft.

Gauthier notes that her gigs teaching songwriting have been some of the most fulfilling experiences for her in recent years. "I started teaching when I was asked to do so at the Rocky Mountain Folks Festival in the early 2000s," she says. "A year later, I went to Costa Rica with Darrell Scott, and we taught together at a yoga retreat center over the Christmas holiday. We did that for a couple years, and the classes just kept growing. I've been teaching on my own several times a year now for about a decade."

Teaching, she adds, "introduces me to

new writers of all ages, allows me to pass on what I have I learned over the years, and keeps me in awe of the alchemy and inspiration that moves a good song into a great song. I love talking about songwriting with songwriters. I get off on it. It is always a joy to bear witness to the divine mystery at work in a songwriter. Inevitably, it makes me feel hopeful and grateful."

No doubt it also provides hope and gratitude to the countless songwriters who have learned from her and others in her position. And, by extension, it provides those things to listeners as

well — something of which Gauthier is well aware.

On the second day of the retreat, she explained the utility of songwriting in plain, empathic terms: A songwriter is not creating something for herself; she's not even creating for the people in the front row who are hanging on her every word. When she sings the word "I," she knows that people aren't thinking "Mary Gauthier," they're thinking about themselves. If you do it right, if you dig deep enough, she said, you can reach "the guy in the back by the fence" who has a car full of empty bottles and a

loaded weapon and a bad idea in his head. He's inches from ending it all, and then he hears your song, and he's breathing easier before he even realizes it.

That is the power of a song, she told her students. That is the goal. Whatever income or notoriety comes is gravy. Write songs for the people you'll never know were moved by what you had to say. Send your songs into the world and let them fly away, then go on to the next one.

It was a powerful statement, which she introduced as "Mary's little speech," to a room full of people who had been

> "I love talking about songwriting with songwriters. I get off on it. It is always a joy to bear witness to the divine mystery at work in a songwriter. Inevitably, it makes me feel hopeful and grateful."
>
> Mary Gauthier

discussing their attempts at performing and stage fright and whether it's worth it to spend money on a fancy producer. It's so easy, when writing songs, to worry about whether your work is pithy or moving enough, to worry over how others might judge you. Meanwhile, if you just tell the truth, people will be moved by the courage of your honesty, and see their own path to their own truth. As I learned during the decade in which I made my way as a songwriter, there's no "creative enough" when one creates. There's just honesty and getting out of the way.

Indeed, perhaps getting out of the way is a good reason to spend a thousand dollars (or more) to travel to another state and sit in a stranger's living room, with other strangers, to create experiences that can inform your songs for years to come. Watching the way other people write, the way they move through a song and their process for doing so, seeing their "old tears" pour out to allow room for new music to fill in, can give a struggling songwriter an idea of how to do all of these things herself. As Gilkyson said, it's a trip to the deep end, and if you've never been there before, it can help to hold someone's hand on the way down. ■

DOING
ALRIGHT

Jason Isbell moves on from the blues

> ## "People call beliefs politics now. You know, they're trying to make them seem smaller, more manageable. Really it's about beliefs."
> Jason Isbell

JASON ISBELL WANTS TO HAVE A word with you. The energetic, consistent, outspoken singer-songwriter and guitarist who grew up in a trailer in rural Alabama is the people's songwriter now, and he has found a way to sing about it all without coming off as preachy, self-righteous, or morbid. That's because he doesn't approach his songwriting as an outsider looking in. "I remember their language and I still speak it," he says of the people he grew up with.

To honor them, Isbell set out to write mini histories of the greater Southern United States. After all, he says, "My job is to talk about people who might be underrepresented in some way."

While many songwriters have spoken for the citizenry — Woody Guthrie killed fascists with his six-string, Johnny Cash spoke openly about the poverty and plight of Native Americans, Joan Baez comforted a nation during a failing war, and Q-Tip and A Tribe Called Quest made us understand what it was like to grow up in Queens — for Isbell, it all comes down to

civility, collective action, and the ability to listen even through disagreement. This last bit, in fact, is something about which he is emphatic. "Once you start yelling, people stop listening," he says. "Civilization — that's what we have to rely on. [We have to] not go back to animals, if we can help it."

As he has throughout his career — with deeply empathic songwriting on "Dress Blues," "Alabama Pines," "Speed Trap Town," "Elephant," and countless others — Isbell dons the clothing of his characters throughout his latest album, *The Nashville Sound* (Southeastern Records, 2017). On the barnburner "Cumberland Gap," he flexes his muscles and lets the lead out with the loudest and saddest coal anthem you've ever heard. With "White Man's World," he deftly turns identity politics into a hummable and thought-provoking radio single. "Hope the High Road" echoes the righteous calls to "go high," not to exhibit our inner demons and bridge trolls.

Indeed, Isbell is no slouch when it comes to the poetry and hard labor of songwriting. Even better, as an instrumentalist, he's capable of lead guitar heroics. He can break your mind with a Bigsby, and break your heart on a dreadnaught. From his early career in the Drive-By Truckers, Isbell made a name for himself as a sort of redneck Jimmy Page. Pair that with a blue-collar family history, years of addiction, and subsequent redemption, and he has a deep well from which to pull.

And now, Isbell is a father to 2-year-old Mercy and devoted husband to singer-songwriter and fiddle player Amanda Shires, which is what matters most. For him, it all comes down to family: the one he grew up in and the one he made, as well as the human family of Alabama musicians, Appalachian coal miners, truck drivers, and Nashville songwriters trying desperately to achieve success while keeping their souls intact in a such a cynical industry.

CAMERON MATTHEWS: Has fatherhood noticeably changed how you approach songwriting or touring?

JASON ISBELL: Yes. It changes everything. Everything. What part would you like me to discuss? Because we can talk about it all day. [Let's] focus on the songwriting aspect.

[My daughter is] 20 months old. What you're looking at right now is somebody who has to learn everything from scratch. If you hand her something to play with, first she has to figure out that it is an object separate from her hand and then she has to figure out that she's supposed to play with it and then she's gotta figure out what to do with it. A lot of those things I think we take for granted. I know for a fact that we do. As grownups, we take those things for granted.

Anything that makes you go back and look at all the steps it took for you to get to where you are emotionally or intellectually, anytime you go back and start looking into those things I think it's really good for any creative pursuit. Especially something like songwriting where … everything's been said before. The only thing you can hope for is a new perspective. If you don't get that from chasing around a person who's a foot tall all day, then you're not doing it right.

CM: Has raising a baby humbled you in any way?

JI: I don't know if she has. I don't know. I grew up in a trailer. When I was Mercy's age I lived in a trailer in my grandmother's yard. So I'm pretty good on the humbling part, you know? After I got sober, I had to apologize to a lot of people for things that I did. If anything, bringing a child home without any kind of manual and keeping her alive for a year and a half has made me the opposite of humble, okay? Ten years ago I couldn't even wipe my own ass.

CM: Your Southern upbringing, your hometown, the people you grew up with are obviously present in your songcraft. Is there somewhere you go in your mind when you sit down to write about them? Do you revisit those childhood places in your mind?

JI: Yes. That's what I'm writing about. I started off my career writing about my family — with a lowercase f. The family that would be now what you would call your extended family, since I've moved out. My parents get the lowercase f at this point in time and my wife and my daughter get the uppercase F. I started out writing songs 15, 20 years ago about my dad, my mom, and my grandparents and things. And then it comes full circle, for lack of a better term. It's come back around where now I'm writing about my own family that I have started with my wife and about how that relates to the family that I grew up around.

Part of me has to exist in those early days, in a trailer in my grandma's yard, and then part of me has to exist now in present time. Memory is a very, very important thing. If you're going to write creatively you have to really be able to take notes without any paper.

CM: A poet friend of mine always says: If you don't mythologize your family, you're doing it wrong.

JI: That makes sense. Because … it's a major shift, when you start seeing your parents as human adults rather than deities. You have this major awakening of, "Holy shit, things were not easy for them and everything they do is not perfect." And then as you get older they go back to being characters in your own story. Which is not always the best way to

"My job is to talk about people who might be underrepresented in some way. And I think that probably lends itself to a journalistic type of writing."

Jason Isbell

treat other people, but that's what happens to our parents and our parents know that. I know that when Mercy's a grown person I'm going to be a cartoon character to her after she's already got over this real fact that I'm a human being and all the digging into my past that she cares to do.

CM: It seems like, in your songs the last few years, you've adapted a specific American experience through personal relationships and writing about your family. And on this record, it seems like you've had kind of like a journalist approach to writing it. Would you say that's true?

JI: I don't know because I've never been a journalist. But you get to a certain point, I think, in your own travels where if you're doing things right and if you're growing as a person, a lot of your problems get solved or at least get closer to being solved, and then it doesn't make a whole lot of sense to write the blues anymore. There's not a whole lot of woe left to share with everybody else, so you have to start finding other things to write about.

I think if you keep the tools sharp and functional and practice a lot and write a lot and work really, really hard ... then you find a way to write about people

who aren't you and do it in a way that is convincing and empathetic. ... I still have my concerns and my worries, and lord knows I have a lot of fears, but for the most part I'm doing alright. I don't think I could sell a story that involves me lamenting my losses at this point in my life because I'm a very happy person.

My job is to talk about people who might be underrepresented in some way. And I think that probably lends itself to a journalistic type of writing.

CM: It's certainly easy to conjure the blues when you're actually living down and out or depressed. Many writers, whether they're poets, novelists, songwriters ... claim that when you're happy the work just doesn't happen. Is this a myth?

JI: Yeah, that's an excuse. That's the people who are telling you, for one reason or another, to keep doing something that's keeping them unhappy. So, if they're drinking a lot, yeah, they'll tell you, 'Oh, if I get happy the work won't be there! Times in my life when I've been happy, I haven't been able to work.' They're telling themselves that lie so they can keep doing whatever it is that's hurting them.

CM: In "White Man's World," one line really stuck out: "Momma wants to

change that Nashville sound, but they're never going to let her." And then I hear a little bit of fiddle there. Can you just talk about that?

JI: Being a white man, there's the white part and there's also the man part. I tried to discuss both of those in that song. Because obviously from my perspective, there's a limited amount of theorizing I can do on race and gender politics or beliefs. People call beliefs *politics* now. You know, they're trying to make them seem smaller, more manageable. Really it's about beliefs.

One of my beliefs is that we're still a very, very long way from making the playing field level for women and men. If you don't believe that, you can look at late night television shows and see how many of the artists that are performing are women. Look at *Saturday Night Live*, women compared to men. Look at your radio charts. What does *Billboard* got right now? Zero women in the top ten? Is that right? I think it is right now.

It's the kind of thing where if I step in and make some statement like: "I'm going to call this record *The Nashville Sound*," anybody's going to look at this and they're going to say ... "That's brilliant. He's taking ownership of this. Blah blah blah. This is really great."

"I don't need everybody to be a fan, it's more important to me to say something that means something. That's how I sleep at night."

Jason Isbell

If a woman were to do the same thing, she wouldn't get the same kind of respect. Women still have to be what my wife calls "available" in this business. By "this business" I don't mean country music in Nashville, I mean [the] entertainment business. [And] America in general, which is, I guess, a business now. Women have to be available in some way to get the same kind of consideration that men get. And I don't have to be. I can be whatever I want to be. As long as my songs are good, people still say that I'm a genius or all this nonsense. When really I just work very hard and I'm lucky. I'm a white male, so the door's always open.

CM: Discussing identity politics in country music is not a common theme these days, though songwriters are attempting to stretch.

JI: It is getting more common. We look at Brad Paisley. I have to salute Brad Paisley for attempting to discuss race with "Accidental Racist." Any time you're writing a song that's going to be called a country song, and it's about race, you're thinking about poor Brad Paisley and the swing-and-a-miss that song turned out to be.

But hey, at least he swung. At least he didn't just stand there and take it. I think

he was trying to start a conversation, and I respect that. But you've got to be real careful. You've got to think real, real hard about what you're going to say if you're a white man with a guitar. People have had about enough of us anyway.

CM: If you look back through the years you can see that there was one other singer-songwriter who had quite a bit of backlash but also a lot of honor in doing what he did: when Johnny Cash wrote about the Native American experience.

JI: Right. That's a funny one to me, you know. A lot of people, not directly discussing Johnny, but a lot of people who I grew up around — people who were real country people, people who like to call themselves rednecks — also think of themselves as Native Americans. And some of them do have some of that blood, some of them don't. They love that dreamcatcher in the rearview mirror of their Camaros. And yeah, the whole of these people have no consideration for ethnic minorities. I don't understand where the disconnect is happening between their idea of the brave and valiant Native American warrior and their idea of the African guy sold into slavery. What's the difference? Why aren't you romanticizing both, if you're going to romanticize one? It's

interesting to me.

The same with Native Americans. You don't have to be as careful because [comparatively] there aren't any of them left. Who you going to piss off? It's a really sad state of affairs. It's hard to have a really positive view of the country that we live in when you start digging too far into the way we treated the people who were here before we were. I think Johnny Cash said what he wanted to say. No matter what the backlash was, I think he said things that he believed in. That's why he turned out to be an icon, even though he didn't write songs and he didn't have a great voice and he wasn't a great musician. His character spoke ...

CM: As a songwriter, how do you tackle the notion that the average music fan doesn't want to dip their tunes into the political mire?

JI: There are different kinds of music. There are people who can sing music for different reasons. Of course you don't want to hear about politics while you're barbecuing with your friends, but that's not what my music is for. I don't need you to listen to this to get worked up for a sports event. That's not what I'm looking for. I don't want as many fans as possible. None of those things make me happy. None of them. I don't want to be in the middle of the room. I'm trying to make art.

They call every single person now who has a record a recording artist. That is a lie. Those people are not artists, for the most part. They shouldn't be called that word. I don't even like to call myself an artist, but my wife has convinced me that that's what I am because I'm not painting the things that I'm making. I'm making them because I feel like they need to be made to make me have enough joy, to make me feel connected to the world. So I make them and I just scatter them out like grass seed.

Whoever wants to pick up on them can. Whoever gets pissed off about them can. That's what art is! That's what it's supposed to be. I don't need CMA awards or ACM awards. I don't need to be respected by my peers. I don't care. I'm here to make rock and roll, because I love working and I'm trying to speak my mind. That's my job. The people who are really fans of the music that I'm making want to give it up.

The people who call it politics are the people who are afraid, somewhere deep down inside, that they might wrong.

CM: There are a lot of younger writers and artists who feel like they can't act like that yet.

JI: Oh, right. But then once you get to a certain age, that part of you is dead.

You think, "I've got to get my foot in the door. I've got to get accomplished. I've got to do something before I tell people *who I am*." The odds of anybody having any kind of success at any kind of creative enterprise are so slim that most people never get to that point. Most people never get out of the lane.

If you do [get success], by the time you've built a little tiny empire for yourself where you can be comfortable and where you can feel comfortable speaking your mind, it's too late! You're old and you're trying to play it safe because you've got families to feed. I'm just never going to play it safe because I've been to a lot of places and I know how many people there are, and I know if I could just sell a record to one tenth of the people in New York City alone then I'll be just fine when it comes time to pay my bills. I don't need everybody to be a fan, it's more important to me to say something that means something. That's how I sleep at night.

CM: The song "Cumberland Gap" really drives the concept of the "other," through a class-based lens. That's not something you hear every day in music.

JI: I feel like I'm lucky enough to have the type of audience who might not only listen to something like that but also might be expanded a little bit by it. I don't have a huge audience. I'm not a big star. I'm not egotistical enough to think that I can change people's minds about it, but that doesn't mean I'm not going to try.

I grew up in a very poor part of Alabama, in a place where the schools were bad and people were working real hard and not seeing a whole lot of anything for it. Then when I got out, I went all over the country and over a great deal of the world. I only live a couple hours away from where I grew up, but I'm in a much nicer neighborhood. I still feel more connected to the people that I grew up around in a small, rural part of Alabama than I do with [the] people with big houses that live in my community.

That's my own hangup. I don't have to reach out to anybody on that side of things. I remember their language and I still speak it. That's not to say that I'm specifically targeting any kind of Trump voters or anything like that. The problem is a lot bigger than that. It's not Trump. Trump doesn't really matter, in all honesty. He's a *symptom*. He's the sneeze. What we've gotta deal with is the virus.

"If you start giving me rules, that's when I really write things. It is kind of a game: Let's see how much of my personality I can get out there without slipping, without stepping off a cliff."

Jason Isbell

CM: Are you worried that maybe the system is just ... rotten?

JI: I'm not afraid of that; I know that for a fact. All of it would be fine if you didn't have people in it. It's just like communism — on paper it's a great idea, and Jesus was a communist. But boy, you start trying to find who's going to run the thing and who's going to make sure everybody's doing what they're supposed to and it immediately gets fucked up beyond repair.

All systems I think of — government policies, financial control, where he's going to put the money — all these things wind up getting really screwed up by greed and fear. Greed is a secondary emotion to fear — fear that you're not going to have enough.

Yeah, it's rotten. It's rotten. Very much so. It was an experiment from the start. I don't know if the American experiment is going to succeed or fail. I'm more concerned with the cultural experiment. I'm happy about the conversations that we're having now: Are the police treating us right? Are black Americans still being kept down because they're black Americans? Are women receiving equal treatment? I think we talk about these things more than we ever have. And we were [talking about them] before the election.

Now, we just got a little bit angrier about it. I love that. That aspect of it is

something that makes me really happy. But, we did fall a couple of steps on the ladder. We didn't fall off the ladder, but we fell a couple of rungs. And now what Amanda calls "the gas station situation" is difficult because assholes have been emboldened.

You see fans at a baseball game yelling the n-word at that Orioles outfielder at Fenway Park this week? I can't help but think to myself, would that have happened if Barack Obama was in the White House? I don't know. Probably. Boston sports fans can be pretty difficult. I feel like the bad behavior has gotten rewarded, so we have fallen back on the ladder a little bit. But we still haven't lost any kind of war, I think.

Culturally, it's impossible for people's minds not to be opened at this point because of the way we exchange information.

CM: Collective action has definitely increased a lot on both sides and I appreciate seeing it in song, for sure. "Hope the High Road" is a really fitting thesis for the entire album. It's positive about politics, and possibly economics as well.

JI: Which can be kind of a tough line to ride. I don't want it to seem like I don't care enough and I don't want it to seem like I'm not angry. Because I am very, very angry, but I don't feel like anger should [triumph] over your dignity. I

think that's the point of that song. No matter how frustrated you are with all this, you're not going to be able to get a whole lot done if you pass that point of diminishing returns.

Once you start yelling, people stop listening. Civilization: That's what we have to rely on. [Let's] not go back to [being] animals if we can help it.

CM: Let's talk a little bit about "Anxiety," the song, and the emotional response that it provokes. Can you paint a picture for me of how that came about? It seems like the length of the track and the song structure could even produce its own bit of anxiety.

JI: Yeah, I guess it could. I think that was part of the point.

That chorus just fell into my lap as I was driving down the road one day worrying about things and analyzing my worry and trying to figure out what was rational and what I could do away with. It was the kind of thing where, as a songwriter, you immediately [question yourself]: "Okay, what can't be real? I have to be overlooking something here. One of these words had to be a gibberish word that my mind's made up and told me it was, or somehow this can't rhyme as well and as easily and as comfortably [as it does]."

[But] sure enough, after I checked back over it a few times that chorus was made up of words in an English language that all came to fit together. It's one of those that's like, I'm just shocked when it's that conversational and it still makes the point and is pointing it in a certain path. I was very happy to do that.

The kind of anxiety that I deal with is not a clinical thing. I don't have anxiety attacks. I don't have panic attacks. I just worry too much, like the Buddy Norris song. I just worry too much. My wife has some experience with the clinical type and so I went to her to help me write the song because I wanted to discuss that as well. I didn't want it to just be restricted to only my experience.

CM: I think you're the first person to ever sing the word "amphibole."

JI: Maybe. I've never heard it in another song. It's a pretty word. It rhymes with coal, which to me is just almost too obvious, isn't it? I almost didn't use that word because it rhymes too cleanly with coal, which was a big topic in the song. I almost thought, I'm just making a new cliché, but I went with it.

CM: Tell me about "Molotov." Why did you choose that image instead of something else that spreads and burns?

JI: Because with a Molotov, if it's made correctly, you know what's usually going to happen. While the thing is still a Molotov, that action hasn't happened yet. Because after that it becomes pieces of garbage. If what you're holding in your hand is a Molotov, that means it hasn't yet exploded. That was how my life was before I straightened it out. I knew what was going to happen and I knew that that was going to make me a completely different thing altogether. That hadn't happened yet. Maybe it's about not quite hitting bottom but [knowing] she's coming.

CM: I really like the weird chord isolation you use in "Chaos and Clothes."

JI: Yeah. That is weird. ... I really wanted something that made me feel like Elliot Smith. ... I had a whole different chorus for that song that did not go to that chord and didn't make you feel a little off-kilter. [But] then I thought, well this is just too pretty and too delicate and too melodic and predictable for what I'm trying to do.

CM: Is "Clothes and Chaos" about anyone in particular?

JI: It's about a few people. I don't want to say real people. I'm not going to call [anyone] out. There's certainly some real characteristics in there. But I never write a song about just one person because that always ends badly.

I started off writing songs about [just] one person but even when they love it, that's kind of the worst possible outcome. Every time you see them you have to play it or talk about it.

CM: I've always been fascinated by your social media chops. Do you just do it for fun or is there part of a career strategy here? What are the up- and downsides to it?

JI: You've got to be really careful. Primary downside is you can make a comment in just a few seconds that can haunt you for the rest of your life if you're not very, very careful.

That being said, I think that format suited me accidentally and naturally. ... I think I'm one of the people who sort of thought in tweets already, if that's possible. ... I've always enjoyed being the guy at the dinner table who can just make a comment and then go back to eating and not have to engage in the conversation. Just say something and then fill my mouth back up.

I like the rules of it. I like the constraints. ... I think a lot of writers think that way. If you start giving me rules, that's when I really write things. It is kind of a game: Let's see how much of my personality I can get out there without slipping, without stepping off a cliff. Which you can do ... in a matter of seconds. It's like being on another planet and not knowing the terrain, and it['s] the middle of the night.

It's beautiful and it's really a lot of fun to communicate with people and get your information that quickly, but goddamn, it's dangerous. Some people shouldn't be allowed to tweet, I think, as we've seen recently. ■

NEVER ENOUGH JOY

The wry humor and raw emotion of Susan Werner's songwriting

by Ron Wray

IN THE WORLD OF SINGER-songwriters, there's no one like Susan Werner. Her songs have covered farm life, religion, Cuba, satire, and more. Werner may not be a household name, but she is respected among her musical peers and has a fierce, cult-like following.

Her songs are often funny without being comedic. One song tells us she smokes cigars and cigarettes, likes plastics, and occasionally votes Republican ("Because I'm Bad"). Another suggests the pesticides she was exposed to growing up on a family farm in Iowa made her, and all her siblings, gay ("Herbicides"). Alongside the humor, Werner delivers songs that hold potential for healing ("May I Suggest") and address current events (like her Trump-driven re-take on "Back in the U.S.S.R."). She can, at once, decimate America's history while lovingly

empowering it ("My Strange Nation").

"If you really want to get to know Susan, you need to see her in concert," says producer Crit Harmon, who has worked with Werner on four albums. "What you see onstage — the humor, the self-deprecation, the sharp-witted political insight — [is] the same thing you get in person. Susan speaks several different languages, not sure how many, but I believe she views music as a language, and the many different genres of music as different dialects that she is constantly learning to speak. She has to be moving forward, turning over the next rock to see what's under it. If it isn't a fresh challenge, she's not interested."

Werner took a message of "evangelical agnosticism" on a tour of both red and blue parts of the country for her 2007 album *The Gospel Truth*, which included the bitingly witty nonbeliever gospel tune "Probably Not" ("Is there a God above? / Is

there eternal love? / Probably not"). Her 2011 release, *Kicking the Beehive,* was a country-styled album produced by Rodney Crowell and featuring Keb' Mo' and Vince Gill. She followed that two years later with an album celebrating the culture of her upbringing in America's heartland — the farm-themed *Hayseed.* Her next project is an EP of songs inspired by a trip to Cuba. And, because why not, she also scored a Broadway-bound musical about baseball based on the film *Bull Durham.*

Casting that wide a thematic net would prove challenging for any songwriter, but Werner is unafraid. In an interview during last February's Folk Alliance International gathering in Kansas City, Missouri, Werner noted, "The biggest challenge of all is to risk writing and singing about what you are a little afraid to write and sing about. Maybe that's sadness. Maybe that's joy. Maybe that's humor. Maybe that's kindness. Maybe that's love. Me, I find it really easy and a total delight to sing other people's songs about great love and kindness — but writing them is like prying teeth. My attempts usually fall over into the ditch of sentimentality — or worse, self-pity. So

there's an Everest left to climb, and I better do it while I still got good knees, right?"

No Need to Explain

Werner was born and raised on a farm near Dubuque, Iowa. After college, she earned a master's in voice from Temple University and was aiming for a life in the opera house. Then she heard Nanci Griffith on the radio and her internal GPS shifted.

"I was writing songs already when I was six or seven, and kept writing through high school and college," she says. "When I got to college, all the music educators were from a tradition, either classical or jazz, and songwriting was viewed as, well, a silly little thing you might do as a hobby but not with any seriousness. So I dropped it.

"[I] went to graduate school, auditioned for operas, got my ass kicked by better, louder singers, got bummed out, started writing songs again, and found some coffee houses in Philadelphia with audiences that actually liked songs — new songs! I couldn't believe it."

Werner eventually landed in Chicago, but remains deeply influenced by the

rural landscapes of her upbringing.

"I love the farmers and growers so much," she says. "[I] love how they talk about the soil and the weather, the language they use — it's so familiar and comforting to me. And it's also a kind of code. Farmers, for the most part, do not share their feelings directly. So if they tell you they're having a good year, they may be telling you something else, like [that] they fell madly in love last month. But they would never tell you that outright. That'd be way too direct, it'd be almost rude.

"I'm attached to that corner of the earth, that landscape, the view of the horizon line in all four directions," she adds. "[That] probably explains my tendency to write in country music forms. That, and the fact that that's what was on Dad's tractor radio. 'When We Get Behind Closed Doors,' 'Harper Valley PTA,' 'Kiss an Angel Good Morning' — that stuff, oh God, I love it."

Along with country songwriting forms, Werner left Iowa with a strong political center, and she veers toward the political in her songwriting from time to time. "Look," she explains, "if you grow up in Iowa, if you live there, the presidential

"The biggest challenge of all is to risk writing and singing about what you are a little afraid to write and sing about. Maybe that's sadness. Maybe that's joy. Maybe that's humor. Maybe that's kindness. Maybe that's love."
Susan Werner

candidates are basically coming right to your front door. Every four years they come by and do their little show. So Iowans are political and cynical, both. Having seen so many politicians come and go, Iowans are educated about the whole process, and they also see right to the bottom of it. ... I met Teddy Kennedy in 1980 in Dubuque, and I'm sure it shaped, or warped, my little mind."

As a result, no topic is too taboo or too political for Werner to address in song. There was a time when she worried about addressing being gay in her songwriting, but it didn't stop her. "You know, I used to fret about it quite a bit," she says. "But we all [fretted about it], didn't we? We were all hung up on categories. Now, I just put the song out there in whatever form it shows up. I don't bother explaining it much.

"I've found that if you don't ask for permission, people tend to assume you know what you're doing," she adds, "and they go with it. It's kind of amazing. 'Oh, that sounds like she's singing as a character who is a guy. Oh, okay.' 'Oh, that sounds like she might be queer. Oh, okay.' 'Oh, that sounds like she might have kids. Oh, okay.' "

Of course folk and roots music songwriting has always been intrinsically political, and part of the folk process suggests writers revive old songs with new lyrics. To that end, Werner recently rewrote her own song, "My Strange Nation," to address our current political predicament.

"[It's] a rewrite of a song I wrote after the 2004 election, when George W. Bush was re-elected," she explains. "I mean, the whole fake WMD deal — and America went for it. Re-elected the guy. [I] couldn't believe it, didn't know what to say, so I wrote a song about it. I mean, that's why we write songs, because we don't know what to say anymore.

"So, Trump wins the election," she adds, "and I started and abandoned about three different songs. Then it came to me that the premise of 'My Strange Nation' still held. ... I'm bewildered by my country, but I'm an American all the way. So I rewrote some of the verses, and, well, what can a songwriter hope for but that their songs speak for other people?"

Though politics is a frequent theme in her songs, so is humor. Many songwriters would shy away from both,

fearing they'd verge either on the preachy or the clownish, but Werner has a knack for balance in her songwriting. Even when toying with difficult topics, she's able to be political without being preachy, silly without being ridiculous.

"Funny songs keep showing up on a regular basis," she says. "[It's] like the way normal, well-adjusted people make a fancy dinner on occasion — to challenge themselves, to delight their friends. I don't fight [those songs] off, I just follow them out.

"Last year," she adds, "I had enough odd ones saved up that I recorded *Eight Unnecessary Songs* — and they are entirely unnecessary, believe me — songs about cosmetic surgery and recumbent bikes and how I'm contributing to global warming. Yet these songs seem to be appreciated more than any other ones right now. People need a laugh. Someone, every day, in every audience, could really use a laugh."

Then, as if to unconsciously advise struggling songwriters, she adds: "I'm figuring that out as I get older: There'll be plenty of sadness, don't worry, you don't have to go looking for it. Aim for some joy — there can never be enough of it." ∎

STOP THINKING, STOP WORRYING

Bravery, feminism, and songwriting advice from Ani DiFranco

by Kim Ruehl

O DiFranco's entire body of work — 19 studio albums across 27 years — and you may begin to understand how songwriting can accompany a person through the world, not just as a sounding board but as a coping mechanism. By leaving no topic off limits, DiFranco has made clear that music is not just here to entertain us, it's here to accompany and support and reinforce our humanity. Our spoken language can connect us to one another, sure. But our musical language can help us understand what it is we want and need to say.

While folk songwriters like Woody Guthrie, Pete Seeger, Bob Dylan, and others certainly never shied from workaday stories and political commentary in their songs, DiFranco has taken the folk idiom further because she has made a point to document a woman's role in the world as well. Early in her career, she did this by leaning hard on youthful outrage, but as the poet has grown, she has included in her writing things Guthrie and Dylan never would have touched: menstruation ("Blood in the Boardroom"), abortion ("Lost Woman Song," "Tiptoe"), and pregnancy ("Landing Gear") among them.

While it's easy to peg DiFranco as a "feminist folksinger," her music is wider than any specific category. She has paired her deeply poetic lyrics with instrumentation that has swung through folk, rock, jazz, punk, and various other forms throughout her career. Her collaborations with jazz players in particular — a long collaboration with jazz bassist and composer Todd Sickafoos and jazz drummer Allison Miller, as well as vibraphonist Mike Dillon, members of Rebirth Brass Band, and now Isaac Neville in some recent performances — have drawn out of DiFranco a certain freedom. Granted, her songwriting has always been a little color-outside-the-lines exploratory, but her determination to weave her folk and punk influences together with jazz has freed what little of her creative energy may have been tethered previously. And it is this aural fearlessness that has solidified her fanbase for going on three decades now.

Indeed, DiFranco's career has shown songwriters everywhere that they can be moved by art, driven by purpose, never get played on the radio, and still make a solid career of music. And that idea is where our recent conversation began. It has been edited for length and clarity.

KIM RUEHL: Instead of being driven by how catchy you can make a song, I get the impression that you've been more driven by how a song can be a vehicle for better understanding, or empathy, or even just exploring ideas. The way you do it is very disarming and vulnerable. How do you get to that? Is that just what comes, or do you do a lot of editing?

ANI DIFRANCO: I think I am just naturally a very vulnerable person in this world, like anybody who's showing themselves through their art. I'm a person who has my heart on my sleeve and my face is like a fucking doorway that anybody can walk through at any moment. I can't seem to hide anything if I try. ...

When I first started songwriting, that was extremely disconcerting to me — showing so much and feeling so naked — but I was just really compelled to do it. Like you say, I wanted to try to communicate or instigate dialogue about things. I just had a really strong will to do that, so I had to acclimate over time to this idea of being extremely vulnerable — not just one-on-one anymore but at the mercy of hundreds or maybe thousands. [I had to be vulnerable to] what they think and how they feel about me, and what I have to say or sing.

I invested a certain amount of bravery early on, [and my career has] really enforced that bravery over time. I've gotten a lot of reactions to what I do, to my heart, but the "thank you" [reaction] that came immediately — that continues to come — hits me so much deeper than the "fuck you, shut up, sit down" [reaction]. It's the people who are like, "Holy shit, yes. That's me too, and I'm so happy you said that," that give my life purpose. That's really reinforced this instinct I had early on that if [I was] brave about my reality, about my truth, about just being myself, then I would relate to a lot more people than would shun me.

KR: I think it gives you some license.

At this point, you've got a lot of years and a lot of records and a track record of being brave, so I'd imagine that it's a little easier now that it's become routine.

AD: Yeah, and it's struck me over the years that I'm kind of a process artist, not a product artist. Like you say, some people invest a lot more in perfection and crafting something catchy. The outcome is in the forefront of their mind.

The art that really compels me is when someone is just in the moment. Whether it results in success or crashing and burning, it's the moment that's compelling to me. It's the risk, you know. I've found over the years that challenging myself to stay in the risk of it all, people have really responded to [that]. Even watching me struggle, watching me fail, watching me explore and end up down blind alleys and have to turn around and come back in my writing and my music. I think all of that

is as much or more interesting than watching the successes.

So I've just thrown songs into the world and some of them are perfection and many of them are not. I think all of the imperfections and all of the stumbling and all of that vulnerability is what people hold more dear.

KR: It's easy to focus on your lyrics when talking about your songwriting, because you're a poet and you nail them. But I think the way your music has evolved over time, from having your guitar front and center to playing with feedback and this huge band, then the vibraphone came in there, and then you started playing with dissonance and release — a lot of that is obviously just what you're drawn to over time, or as you grow older. But how much of that has been intentional, searching for the perfect sound or the right vibe?

AD: I think that what turns me on,

inside, is the unexpected. When I'm making music, I almost shy away from the catchy, predictable chorus or the gratifying, expected moment. My tendency is to crank the wheel and take a left turn.

Just because that excites me, I find that the melodies or the music I've made that's more predictable or standard in its progressions or its constructions are songs that I don't want to play as much. I get bored with them. To keep myself interested, I try these different things. What those things are is so influenced by my influences, which could be the musicians I'm working with and/or the music that they're listening to, [that they] bring into my life, or the record I'm super enraptured by, or the whole genre of music that just unfolded before me. Like many artists, I'm kind of a sponge. Everything that excites me enters my body and then comes out in

"Until human beings start putting this language into music, it will never be perceived as musical or possible. Somebody's got to do it! It's just one way that I try, through my art, to be a part of the solution."

Ani DiFranco

some way.

It's really not heady — it's not of the head or mind for me; it's instinct. When you see the different musical places I've gone, you can just see where my heart was at the time.

KR: I was thinking about an interview that we did years ago, during the Bush administration, when I asked you why you thought more singer-songwriters weren't parading out the protest songs. At the time you said they're hard to write and it's hard to make the language of what's wrong sound musical. I remember you specifically called out the word "patriarchy" as hard to sing, but you've used it since then.

AD: I have! [Laughs.]

KR: It shows up again on "Play God," on *Binary*. Do you think we've just gotten to a point where the inherent musicality of a word is less important than the need to use it?

AD: Well, I mean, I guess I got to that point a long time ago.

On this new record, there's a song called "Alrighty" that's about patriarchy but it doesn't use the word. It uses very simple language.

But with a song like "Play God," I pushed even further. Until human beings start putting this language into music, it will never be perceived as musical or possible. Somebody's got to do it! It's just one way that I try, through my art, to be a part of the solution.

I still ache for more company in political songwriting, for information [for] myself. I still feel exactly like I did when we spoke, that conversation you referred to. I'd say the same thing right now, although it does seem like now there is more of a groundswell of artists that are trying to rise to that, [who are trying to] get political, speak to something, be part of the resistance in

their art, which really excites me. I can't wait to hear other people's ideas about how it's done.

I guess I just have always tried to be the change, as they say.

KR: When I heard that this record was going to be called *Binary*, I immediately expected commentary on traditional gender roles, given the trans rights conversation, but it's even more ambitious than that. What's the overarching message you're going for?

AD: I guess the overarching message that comes through that poem, and the whole record — which is why that poem's title is titling the record — is a feminist message. To my mind, a central tenet of feminism is prioritizing "relationship" and holding it higher than everything else that is typically what women do, to generalize.

Of course, we all have the feminine and the masculine, and it's not really about men and women as much as it is about mediating the masculine with the feminine, and having them be equally balanced in the design of our societies and governments and cultures. We can all, no matter what our gender, participate in that or participate in patriarchy. But I think feminism is the mechanism that we have to address patriarchy.

Disease is the result of imbalance, in whatever context you find it. And patriarchy is a fundamental imbalance in all of human society, from which I think the result will always be social, political disease. We've really got to begin at the beginning with this.

The way that I think and [the way that I] look at things, and the amount of time in my life I've spent meditating on feminism, on patriarchy, has made the idea of "relationship" more and more central to my thinking. I look at the whole world, and I see it as binary concepts repeated everywhere, whether it's planets and stars or masculine and feminine or positive and negative, the very atomic structure.

There's no such thing as singularity. I'm so intrigued by quantum physics, the way that science, at its vanguard, has come around to some very essential understandings, [that] nothing exists except as a field of possibilities, until it's perceived. Perception is synonymous with interaction, and interaction is what creates existence. That's how we *exist*, is in relationship.

I think we need to bring some fundamentally feminist concepts to the table in order to get out of here.

So "Binary" — I never say the word "feminism" or "patriarchy" in that poem, but I'm trying to get to a really fundamental basis for addressing those things.

Like, let's talk about this idea of a hierarchy of individuals. That's not untrue and it exists, but ... along with a hierarchy of individuals, we have to hold up a network of relationship equally [as] high and talk about the world through both of those lenses, to get to any truth or any answers to any questions.

KR: What have your kids taught you about your art?

AD: That's funny you should ask, because when we were talking about process versus product, I was going to go off on a tangent about my kids, watching them make art, and how they are all the way there. I attempt to recapture my child mind and my total presence and being in the moment when I'm making art, but they really do it. It's so instructive and so inspiring to watch. ...

I have a 10-year-old and a 4-year-old. Both of them, when they're drawing or painting, it's amazing to watch someone make marks that have no intention. They have no ideas about where it should go ... there's no calculation. It's just all visceral.

When I'm drawing with my kids, I look at my marks and I'm like, oh, self-conscious overthought lines [versus] totally free, visceral, from-your-spleen lines. You can see the difference. It's amazing.

My daughter is way into music and it's so interesting to hear her sing because she really takes risks and gets it wrong all the time without knowing or caring, and then when she gets it right it's like, "Holy shit!" You see God.

She's becoming quite this harmony singer. When we drive to and from school, she plays music and sings along with everything. It's so amazing to watch her explore melody and harmony with this freedom that I'm attempting to achieve in any moment. And [for] a kid, it's fucking automatic. They're great teachers about how to free your voice, free your expression: Stop thinking, stop worrying, stop calculating. ■

FEELING FREE

Samantha Crain breaks out of a musical box

by Jonathan Bernstein

PHOTOS BY DAKOTA LEWALLEN

In the fall of 2016, Samantha Crain sat in an Oakland, California, recording studio trying to figure out how to start over.

It wasn't the first time. For the previous five years, she had been traveling to the Bay Area from her native Oklahoma to make records with John Vanderslice, the producer known for his penchant for pushing singer-song-writers toward more experimental sounds and styles. That approach is what first attracted Crain to Vanderslice, who has produced three of her albums — *Kidface* (2013), *Under Branch & Thorn & Tree* (2015), and *You Had Me at Goodbye* (2017). Putting a different twist on the singer-songwriter model was always the goal for Crain and Vanderslice, but while working on *You Had Me*, Crain was convinced that her efforts hadn't yet gone far enough. She was determined to really shake things up, to declare a hard break with the straightforward folk approach that had formed the core of her artistry since she first began making music as a college student.

To set the direction, she brought a new song to Vanderslice called "Smile When" — a brisk pop tune about the fleeting thrills of lovesickness. Vanderslice had an idea to try recording the song with just bass, drums, and vocals. He kept asking her questions,

running new ideas by her: If the bridge isn't quite working, he would suggest, why don't we add an out-of-tempo Minimoog synthesizer? "That sounds insane," Crain recalls telling him, much in the same way that she's responded to most of Vanderslice's offbeat proposals. "But let's do it."

Granted, saying yes to this kind of free-wheeling experimentation has been a decade-long process for Crain. Soon after releasing her debut EP, *The Confiscation*, in 2007 at the age of 21, she was hailed by many as Oklahoma's wunderkind folk troubadour. ("A mature sound, womanly rather than girlish," read a cringeworthy review in *PopMatters*. "Writing and vocal skills beyond her years," stated *The Oklahoman*.) Her reputation only solidified when she followed *The Confiscation* with two full-length albums: *Songs in the Night* (2009) and *You (Understood)* (2010).

When critics lauded Crain's wise-beyond-her-years self-seriousness, the praise made such a big impression on the young singer that she spent the better part of the next decade trying to live up to it, and then break free from it.

"I basically spent the majority of my young adulthood taking myself very seriously," Crain said over the phone from her home in Norman, Oklahoma,

> "The fact that people can't personally name any Native musicians that are making contemporary music is actually the whole point. The whole point is being able to say, 'I'm making contemporary, modern music, and I'm a Native American, and I also have a deep connection to my heritage and want to bring that out into the mainstream.'"
> Samantha Crain

last spring. "Everyone started giving me this label of being an old soul, and because I was really young and I didn't have a good idea of who I actually was, I just grabbed ahold of that label. I let it direct my songwriting and my demeanor, and my aesthetic in general, because I wanted to live up to that expectation."

By teaming up with Vanderslice, Crain was looking for ways to change course. But the transformation has been gradual.

Trying On Tradition

Crain and was born and raised in Shawnee, Oklahoma, a small city 40 miles east of Oklahoma City. Apart from a brief stint living in London, she's lived in Oklahoma for most of her life, attending college in Shawnee, later living in Oklahoma City, and now residing 30 miles south of the city in Norman, where she's lived for the past four years.

Growing up as a child with Native ancestry, Crain devoured encyclopedias and books of Choctaw hymns at her grandmother's house. "Some of the first singing I ever heard was going to powwows or hearing drum groups," she

told *Indian Country Today* in 2012. Yet when Crain would find her way to writing her own songs as a teenager, she was drawn to the plaintive folk of singer-songwriters like Neil Young and Joni Mitchell.

She began making her own music shortly after graduating high school. She spent several years in college writing short stories and turning them into song sketches. When she released *The Confiscation*, in 2007, she subtitled it *A Musical Novella,* hinting at how closely related prose and songwriting were for her.

But it was her Vanderslice-produced 2013 breakthrough, *Kidface* — a stark, lo-fi acoustic record — that displayed a songwriter hitting her stride. The disc relied on 1960s-style recording techniques — no reverb, no tape delay, less dynamic spacing. The result was a shocking directness that garnered the attention of a wider national audience and established Crain as one of the most promising young voices in heartland roots music. It earned praise from mainstream critics in *Rolling Stone* and *NME*, and Crain began traveling to Europe for extensive tours.

As soon as she started receiving heightened attention and publicity, Crain

began using her platform to point out injustice and speak her mind on social issues that affected local communities in Oklahoma. In 2014, she organized a protest at the Norman Music Festival as the governor's daughter, Christina Fallin, performed with her band Pink Pony in full Native American headdress. The protest drew a great deal of media coverage, resulting in an apology from Governor Mary Fallin. Two years later, Crain vocalized her frustration online with the alarming gender disparity at Medicine Stone — an eastern Oklahoma red-dirt music festival that had booked just one woman-fronted act in its first four years.

"I assume I've lost fans with some of the stances I've taken on things," Crain told the *Alaska Dispatch News* in 2015. "But that's not really worrisome to me."

Nonetheless, as Crain's reputation for outspokenness and folkie wisdom has grown, she notes, "I feel like I missed out on a lot of the freedom that comes with making art as a young person." And it's that fact that drove her to work with Vanderslice as she has tried to remodel her entire philosophy around music, treating it as something freeing and creative for creativity's sake, something fun.

For his part, Vanderslice notes, "I'm more into the headspace where if there's going to be any production happening on a record, it needs to be a little off. You're making a movie, instead of putting on a play. And because I'm a weird dude, that movie is going to be more like a David Lynch movie."

A New Approach

In 2015, Crain turned again to Vanderslice for her *Under Branch & Thorn & Tree* album. Despite its arresting songwriting and outside-the-box production, it did little to convince listeners that Crain wasn't a deeply committed folksinger intent on breaking hearts and telling bleak stories in her music. Though Vanderslice added elegant string sections and more ornately produced arrangements to Crain's sonic template, the disc, a collection of expertly woven storytelling ("Elk City") and devastating moments of existential alienation ("If I Had a Dollar"), in fact represented the apex of Crain's folk artistry. It was a great effort, but by that point, she had spent eight years writing such songs on her acoustic guitar. As far as she was concerned, they were all beginning to sound similar.

Though *Under Branch* was well received and Crain continued to tour, back home she was struggling to make ends meet as a full-time touring musician, picking up jobs whenever she was off the road. In order to finance the recording of her next album, Crain spent two years working 60-hour weeks as a waitress in Norman. And she started writing again, turning to a mini keyboard and synthesizer instead of her acoustic guitar.

"Basically, I just felt like I had become a little bit lazy," she says. "I had been feeling like all of my songs were starting to sound the same. I knew that in the past, whenever I've ... used an electric guitar, or moved over to the piano, which I've done a few times in the past, I've ended up writing differently. It just changes up the way that your brain is thinking about melody.

"When I sit down to play an acoustic guitar, my hands want to do the same thing, because I've been playing guitar for so long," she explains. "They want to play a certain chord or chord progression, because it's comfortable, and it's muscle memory. But when you put a new instrument in front of you, you don't have those habits in place. I'm not super proficient on piano, so it frees me

up to write purely based on melody and not so much based on chord progressions."

One can hear Crain's newfound sense of playful experimentation on the resulting disc, this year's *You Had Me at Goodbye* — a quirky, off-kilter indie-pop record grounded in intricate, meandering melody. There, Crain confounds genre expectations to great effect — replacing strumming guitars with cellos, deploying clarinets as lead instruments, favoring fuzz guitar over pedal steel.

"There are a lot of ideas we messed with on the past couple records I did with John that I was afraid ... to take all the way," Crain says. "This time, though, I really didn't have a problem taking a lot of those recording ideas and weird synthesizer things and just going as far as we could with them. This album is definitely taking stuff that I've been slowly getting comfortable with over the past couple albums and feeling a lot more freedom to utilize those things in a more complete way."

Last spring, Crain created a Spotify playlist of artists that had inspired the making of *You Had Me at Goodbye* and posted it online. Missing from that list were her long-established songwriting heroes like Neil Young, Woody Guthrie, and Buffy Sainte-Marie. Instead, the list was much more contemporary, more pop-leaning, more eclectic: Jon Brion, D'Angelo, Cyndi Lauper, Harry Nilsson, and Beyoncé.

"It's been a real joy to watch Samantha ... uncover new rocks and see what there is under them," says James Phillips of Bombadil, Ramseur Records labelmates with whom Crain has toured over the years. "It's really exciting to hear her using more electronic sounds and more angular approaches to production and instrumentation on this new record. Her last few albums were really great, but they were pretty much straightforward folk records. This album is really stretching the boundaries of what a singer-songwriter/folk artist can do."

You Had Me embodies Crain's sense of levity. There's an off-kilter humor and breezy stream of consciousness that weaves its way through the record's ten songs, most evidently on album opener "Antiseptic Greeting," a song about, among other things, being overwhelmed by choices at a grocery store. In the song, Crain narrates with deadpan paranoia: "Doing a crossword at the café, and all of a sudden I'm overcome with worry about whether or not I'm pregnant or just stressed out." There are far more jarring details on this record, a sign that as a songwriter, Crain has adopted more of an absurdist realism, embracing the specificity of life's random, goofy quirks instead of trying to create an idealized reality for herself.

"I tried to inject myself a little bit more into the songs," she says. "I have a weird sense of humor and I feel okay trying new things, so I was just trying to encompass myself more instead of [trying to encompass] some idea of who people think I am.

"I feel like I have a certain sense of levity ... with music," she adds later. "That comes with getting more comfortable with [my]self and getting older. It's not really something that I could have done other than now, having made all the records I've made up until this point."

One of the highlights on *You Had Me* is "Red Sky, Blue Mountain," the first song Crain has ever recorded in Choctaw. Having spent time touring and performing in Canada, Crain has gradually become exposed to a more fully formed community of indigenous and aboriginal folk music traditions. With age, she's become increasingly curious about her own indigenous musical heritage, so when she set out to write her most recent album, she felt particularly compelled to write a new original song for her people. For help with the language, she reached out to Dora Wickson, translation specialist at the Choctaw Nation of Oklahoma. Crain sent Wickson lyrics she had written about natural beauty being disrupted by the material world:

The red sky
A blue mountain
The dream that is real
Born to change the world
And we did
But what have we done?

"Samantha has a big platform," says Wickson, who was thrilled to get the opportunity to help Crain translate the song. "My job is to try to help keep the language alive, so I'm always trying to help someone like Samantha. My hope is that they'll take it and run with it."

Indeed, "Red Sky, Blue Mountain" was the first in a series of new songs that Crain has been writing in Choctaw. "A very important way in which language gets immortalized and passed on is by putting it to song," says Crain, who believes

strongly in the importance of creating new indigenous art, though she's encountered some objections within the Choctaw community, whose members believe that Native artists should only perform and teach music that's been passed down for centuries.

"The only way to keep these cultures growing and keep them alive is to keep adding to them and facing those fears that people have of new art created within the culture not being legitimate," she continues. "The fear of new indigenous art really needs to be looked at head-on. People need to get over that so that young artists and musicians growing up in that culture and in these tribes will feel comfortable making their own art and will also feel comfortable calling it Choctaw art."

Crain feels all the more duty to lend her perspective, as a Choctaw artist, to the larger world of modern roots music. When I ask if she feels like there are other young Native artists who, like her, are making modern roots music, she turns the naïve question into a teachable moment. "The fact that people can't personally name any Native musicians that are making contemporary music is actually the whole point. The whole point is being able to say, 'I'm making contemporary, modern music, and I'm a Native American, and I also have a deep connection to my heritage and want to bring that out into the mainstream.'"

She points to The Band's Robbie Robertson as an example of an artist with Native ancestry (he is half-Mohawk) who never made public his background until long after The Band's commercial peak in the '70s. "He probably didn't feel like anybody cared about that part of him," Crain suggests. "The goal is bringing this kind of thing to a point where it can just co-exist with anything else, which is important,

accompanying physical ailments, Crain needed to press pause.

"I find myself having to regroup," she wrote. "I need to find out who I am outside of being a touring musician because I know, deep down, that isn't what defines me. It's just a thing I love to do, but it's also a thing that destroys me, because it doesn't allow me to take care of myself. And that's fine, I'm not entitled to success or to make a living playing music. I hoped that I could, but now I realize that I can't, at least not right now."

After mining emotional experiences and painful memories for her songs for the entirety of her adult life, Crain needed to take stock of the toll that her music and art had taken on her. Faced with the overwhelming financial and professional pressures to be constantly creating, stopping to reflect on one's own well-being is not an easy decision for any artist to make, but it can often be a necessary one.

"I'll be fine eventually," Crain told me, with the calm assurance of someone getting the hang of prioritizing her own mental and physical health. Indeed, within just a few months of canceling her tour, Crain had announced a short fall tour opening for the Mountain Goats.

Perhaps as Crain continues to take more time to reflect on the trials of working as a professional singer-songwriter, and as she continues to take care of herself and her own well-being, she'll feel more free than ever, eventually, to create and craft art without the pressures and restrictions that come with treating one's art as a full-time job. Earlier this year, before *You Had Me* was released, she candidly noted, "I'm just kind of at the point in my life where there's no point in making art if it doesn't try to stick out in some way. Because otherwise I'm just making noise — and there's enough noise." ∎

especially with people's obsessions with American roots music. If you're going to have all of this stuff about American roots music but you don't ever include the actual roots of the roots ..."

Crain stops her thought short. She knows she's already made her point.

Pressing Pause

Just over a month after the March 2017 release of *You Had Me At Goodbye*, Crain announced that she was canceling her entire upcoming East Coast tour for personal reasons. When I heard this news, I reached out to her to ask if she'd be willing to talk. A few days later, she sent me an email:

"I've never canceled a tour in my 11 years of touring, so it's sort of a lot of things all conspiring together," she wrote. She went on to explain that, after repressing various personal tragedies over the past few years, she had been having mental health problems. A month after the release of her creative rebirth of an album, she was distraught over its meager reception. "Nobody bought it or cared about it," she wrote. Ticket sales for her upcoming tour were so low that she was unsure if she would have been able to pay her band on tour. Deep in debt, mired in a mix of personal trauma, political anxiety, and

Thoughts on Five Great Songs

words by Colin Hay
illustrations by Jenny Ritter

I was still living in Scotland when this Beatles song pounced into my life. I found it totally captivating: The sound of the drums, the part that Ringo played, the rich, lustrous instrumentation, the meandering weave of the melody, and the brilliance of the lyrics, which created a world to which I so wanted to belong.

Living is easy with eyes closed
Misunderstanding all you see

The first time I heard this song, written by Joni Mitchell but made famous by Judy Collins, I loved it. For someone to write about the realization that so much of life is unknowable was pure wisdom. Is Joni Mitchell the greatest songwriter ever? She may well be.

I've looked at love from both sides now
From give and take and still somehow
It's love's illusions I recall
I really don't know love at all

Who would have thought to put these lyrics in a song? Only Chuck Berry, because he was classical in his own right. He wrote the book on rock and roll, and it deserves to be read, time and time again.

My heart beatin' rhythm
and my soul keep a-singin' the blues
Roll over Beethoven
and tell Tchaikovsky the news

It's Bob Dylan's fault; he's the one who made us believe.

This song jauntily bounces along, with immaculate poetry supported by revolutionary instrumentation, which became a template of sorts for rock-and-roll bands from then on. Drums, bass, guitars, and the glue of the B3 organ — it all rolled along majestically for over six minutes, and we never wanted it to stop. May it never.

You say you never compromise
with the mystery tramp, but now you realize
he's not selling any alibis
as you stare into the vacuum of his eyes
and say, "Do you want to make a deal?"

This song from The Kinks is about yearning and the idea that paradise exists in simplicity, for the song's characters Terry and Julie, as well as for you and me. It's about home being indeed where the heart is.

The lead guitar line is devastatingly simple and completely beautiful. The chordal structure is also simple but always interesting. Ray Davies' vocal delivery carries the emotions of countless generations of Londoners, bathed in the comforting glow of that sunset.

Every day I look at the world from my window
But chilly, chilly is the evening time
Waterloo sunset's fine

NOT JUST BIDIN' HIS TIME

Five decades into a storied music career, Chris Hillman finds he has more to say

by David McPherson

L to R: John Gray, Chris Hillman, and Herb Pedersen

> ## "I had no intention of ever recording again. It happened haphazardly and fell into my lap. When we least seek something out, it usually happens."
> Chris Hillman

IT WOULD BE EASY FOR septuagenarian songwriter Chris Hillman to live quietly, perform a few shows here and there, and collect past record royalties from his work as a co-founder of The Byrds and a member of the Flying Burrito Brothers, Manassas, and the Desert Rose Band. Thankfully for all of us with ears, that scenario has not come to pass.

Hillman's passion for performing is unwavering. He feels blessed to still do what he loves and have an audience that cares. "That's how you measure your worth as you get older," he said in a recent interview, "as long as you can reach some semblance of [the] efficiency you reached in your younger days." At 72, as long as there are fans still eager to hear Hillman, he's happy to oblige.

Artists as diverse as Roy Rogers, Tom Petty, Emmylou Harris, Beck, and Scottish hard-rockers Nazareth have recorded songs written by Hillman over the past four decades. Earlier this fall, he hit the road to promote his new record, *Bidin' My Time*, which he

released in September on Rounder Records. The project was a bit of a fluke; but, oh boy, what a lucky strike. Hillman's voice is still silky and smooth. On the 12 cuts, he channels his long-gone comrades-in-song from The Byrds and the Flying Burrito Brothers (Gene Clark and Gram Parsons, specifically) to offer compositions old and new that linger with the listener.

"I had no intention of ever recording again," Hillman says of his first batch of new recordings in over a decade. "It happened haphazardly and fell into my lap. When we least seek something out, it usually happens.

"It is not a concept album," he adds, "but there is some bluegrass, some country, and some rock ... covering all my history well and touching on a lot of bases."

Bidin' My Time takes listeners to another stratosphere. Once there, you are left in a pleasant place where you long to stay. It's a record full of sonic layers. Yet it's sparse, not overproduced, and allows Hillman's voice to shine. Featured performers and guests on the recording include Byrds co-founders David Crosby and Roger McGuinn; Desert Rose Band alumni Herb Pedersen, John Jorgenson, and Jay Dee

Maness; Petty and fellow Heartbreakers Mike Campbell, Steve Ferrone, and Benmont Tench; Mark Fain, Josh Jové, and Punch Brothers' Gabe Witcher.

The disc kicks off with a new recording of Pete Seeger's and Welsh poet Idris Davies' "The Bells of Rhymney," which the Byrds recorded for their 1965 debut, *Mr. Tambourine Man*. Crosby and Pedersen add gorgeous harmonies to the song. "It took us three or four hours," says Hillman, "and Herb worked David really hard; he looks up to him as a fellow tenor singer."

"The Bells of Rhymney" is a song Hillman always wanted to record. "It starts out acoustically and builds from there," he explains. "When The Byrds cut it on our first album, it was the song that best described who we were as a band. It's also always been my favorite song we ever recorded."

Cowboy Chords

Hillman grew up in California, 40 miles from the Mexican border, dreaming of a career in music. Born in 1944, he is a proud third generation Californian. His great-grandfather arrived in what was then the Wild West by wagon train and horseback in 1884. When Hillman was a teen, his mother made him a deal: She would help him get his first guitar, and if he stuck with it for one year, she would help him get another one. A trip to Tijuana resulted in his first instrument; his mom's $10 investment paid off in spades.

Hillman quickly learned the basic cowboy chords and started to strum and sing. Television played a role as he learned more; he was fascinated by the live music shows that broadcast from L.A. "I watched Spade Cooley every Saturday night," he recalls, "along with Ranch Party and Cal's Corral."

After his sister, whom he calls "the bohemian of the family," came home from college with a stack of Pete Seeger, Woody Guthrie, and Lead Belly records, Hillman — then a teenager — fell in love with folk music. (Old-time music and bluegrass came soon after.)

Then, just as Hillman was launching his music career, his father committed suicide. That's a lot for anyone to take, let alone a 16-year-old. Hillman discovered a lot of anger, and channeled it into his instrument. It may also have fueled him getting into the rock-and-roll lifestyle of drugs and excess, but fortunately he did not indulge in the way that some of his friends did. "I made some bad choices in the rock-and-roll lifestyle, believe me," he says. "But I never crossed that line. For a lot of my friends, music became secondary as a career; for me, the pursuit of pleasure became the career."

Heading into high school, Hillman and his guitar rarely parted. The budding musician started taking lessons every Saturday afternoon from the head custodian at his school, who played in a country and western band. Apart from showing him chords, his teacher also played him records. It was through those lessons that he discovered Buck Owens and the Bakersfield sounds for the first time, along with Lefty Frizzell and Webb Pierce.

Head down, ears open, fingers suddenly itching inexplicably for a mandolin, this Southern California kid's obsession soon latched onto Appalachian familial harmonies and strings, changing the course of SoCal music and the broader field of American pop in the 1960s.

Joining the Rodeo

In 1968, when The Byrds released their sixth album, *Sweetheart of the Rodeo,* it

Chris Hillman, left, with Herb Pedersen.

caught many by surprise. It was a groundbreaking, genre-bending cocktail of sounds not easily understood by longtime fans. Mainstream Nashville was not impressed with these hippies invading their musical territory. Even though it received some favorable reviews, the album peaked at No. 77 on Billboard's LP chart in the US, and didn't even enter the UK charts. The broader music industry shook its head in bewilderment.

The addition of songwriter and multi-instrumentalist Gram Parsons swerved the California group into a left turn from its previous psychedelic-folk sound. In the ensuing decades, *Sweetheart* has become a seminal record. It helped pave the way for bands such as Poco, Dillard & Clark, and later the Eagles. The album is also one to which many of today's Americana stars point as a touchstone for the genre and an inspiration. Fifty years on, the songwriting still resonates.

It was around the time of *Sweetheart* when Hillman's songwriting emerged. Following a studio session with McGuinn, playing for a young South African jazz player who complimented his bass playing, Hillman went home and wrote his first song, "You and Me."

Previously, the only tune the musician had composed was a bluegrass instrumental. In 2009, Hillman told an audience at a Library of Congress lecture, "It was like the cobwebs had come off of me. The songs just started pouring out. At that moment in my life, the door started swinging open and I started writing and singing more."

Until then, he'd been content as just a player, but for The Byrds' *Younger Than Yesterday* sessions he brought several songs, including the gorgeous "Have You Seen Her Face." As Roger McGuinn told *American Songwriter* in a 2010 interview, ten years following the release of *Younger Than Yesterday*,

"Chris was a late bloomer. But when he bloomed, he blossomed."

Asked about the importance of The Byrds, the Burritos, Parsons' influence, and *Sweetheart of the Rodeo* in particular in ushering a new genre, Hillman is both humble and nostalgic for those magical groups he played a role in 50 years ago.

"It's funny," he says. "With the Burrito Brothers, we couldn't even get arrested! We were lazy in our execution. The songs were great and Gram Parsons was a great co-writer, but we couldn't get on country radio, nor could we get on early FM rock radio. We were edgy and just having a good time. Now, we are revered, in a sense.

"Our royalties were in the red for so many years and now we are in the black," he adds. "[We're] selling more copies of these records today than we were when we were together. Bernie Leadon and I are the only ones left now. It was such an odd band and so interesting. I tell people it was like being in a Mexican circus for three years."

Alternative Country

On a recent morning, Hillman was driving down the L.A. Freeway when "Dark End of the Street" by the Bee Gees came on the radio. It got him thinking of his lost songwriting soulmate Parsons. "Gram and I used to sing that song," he says, "but we twisted it so it was told from the man's point of view. It was alternative country in that sense.

"*Sweetheart of the Rodeo* opened a lot of doors for us; it was a noble experiment. I'll admit, it's not my favorite record, but Gram brought in two beautiful songs: '100 Years from Now,' and 'Hickory Wind.' Gram was hungry, ambitious, and going for it at that time; then he started to drift away."

Yet, in 1969, as The Byrds broke apart, Hillman partnered with Parsons and started the Flying Burrito Brothers. This period saw some of Hillman's most storied songs emerge, many of them co-written with the cosmic cowboy.

"Gram and I were sharing a house and writing songs together every day," Hillman recalled during his Library of Congress lecture. "We were very close, like brothers, for that year and a half. We wrote songs like 'Sin City.' 1969 was the end of it all. Things were starting to fall apart with the Manson murders, Woodstock, campus unrest, and protests against Vietnam. It was as close to anarchy as our country has ever reached." Yet, as is true of so many timely and timeless songs, as we've seen unrest sweep through towns like Ferguson, Missouri, and Charlottesville,

Virginia, more recently, "Sin City" seems as relevant now as ever.

Though time changes so much even as so much remains the same, talking with Hillman today, it becomes clear that he is grateful for every experience.

"I don't know if I'll ever make another record, to be honest, but this was a really great experience," Hillman says of the *Bidin' My Time* sessions. "[Producer] Tom [Petty] is a wonderful guy ... he just loves music. His longevity and his commitment are so admirable. Just think of the Heartbreakers. Those guys have been together for 40 years. How many bands can we count that have been together that long? It really speaks volumes about Tom. He is a very humble guy."

The two were connected by mutual friend Herb Pedersen, who was touring with Petty and cooked up some plans while they were out on the road. By the time they got off that tour, Pedersen and Petty were both convinced another album had to be in the cards for Hillman. Pedersen called his friend and

"Gram and I were sharing a house and writing songs together every day. We were very close, like brothers, for that year and a half."
Chris Hillman

said, "You still have some songs lying around, don't you? I'm going to meet with some labels."

"I had no aspirations of anything beyond recording some songs ... I wasn't chasing a career," Hillman insists. "I had a couple of songs lying around and a couple other ideas and told [Tom], 'You might not like them.' ... Tom played harmonica on one song and guitar on 'Here She Comes Again.' Overall, he was just there ... a good cheerleader. He was never nitpicking. Rather, he told me to just go for it!"

Bidin' and Blessed

The dozen tracks on *Bidin' My Time* are a pleasant mix of new compositions, re-recordings, and fresh takes on old tunes ("New Old John Robertson" and "Here She Comes Again"), and a Petty cover ("Wildflowers") thrown in for good measure. The title track is something from 1987. "It would have been on a Desert Rose album, but never made it," Hillman says. "It reminds me

of an early Burritos cut."

The newest song ("Such Is the World We Live In"), written a year and a half ago, is as close as Hillman — who jokes, "Next to Ted Nugent, I might be one of the only conservatives in the Rock and Roll Hall of Fame!" — gets to addressing politics. The tune was co-written with Hillman's friend Steve Hill, with whom he has gotten together every so often over the past 20 years to write songs. Driven by some tasty mandolin, the song is a breezy, front porch-style jam fueled by thoughtful lyrics:

I never thought I would see the day
*   when America was on the run*
Not sure what they're
*   running from ...*
No darkness will hold us down
No empty words will make a sound

We will be together again
Such is the world that we live in.

"It's [about] how I was feeling when I wrote this song, in a political, cultural sense," Hillman explains. "I don't believe any musician or actor should steer the crowd into their political philosophy. Instead, it's written from the point of view of someone's great-grandfather who is saying to us everything wrong now is right. It's a jab at how our cultural norms have been turned upside down. I wasn't judging. I was just asking, what's really going on here?"

Whether one likes this collection of songs or not is not the main concern. What matters is that Hillman took a chance and put these tunes out there.

"What do we all want?" he asks. "We want approval. That's one of the negatives of the human condition, but I'm not going to bother with that. I'm not betting my entire existence on if I get approval for *Bidin' My Time*. I'm just happy we did it, and I feel blessed." ■

COL 68556

BOB DYLAN TIME OUT OF MIND

A NEW DIMENSION OF AMERICANA

Daniel Lanois on Bob Dylan and Willie Nelson

by Stephen Deusner

IN THE MID-1990S, DANIEL LANOIS produced three albums in a row where he drew from the past while seeing into the future. It was a time pre-*O Brother*, when alt-country was rising alongside gritty interpretations of rock and folk music, and Lanois was teaming up with titans of American music to create a loose Americana trilogy.

In the Fall 2017 issue of *No Depression,* I began to delve into those three discs, discussing Emmylou Harris' 1995 album *Wrecking Ball* with Lanois in depth. He followed that project two years later with Bob Dylan's *Time Out of Mind,*

which played like a commentary on the songwriter's vast catalog, full of cryptic lyrics, doomsday imagery, and grooves that sound like they're propelled by the weight of American history. It sounds like an old memory of that "thin, wild mercury" sound Dylan crafted in the 1960s, itself a response to the conservative strictures of folk music. Arguably the most pivotal record in Dylan's later career, *Time Out of Mind* was hailed as a comeback, and it heralded a period of renewed relevance and rejuvenated creativity in the 21st century. Dylan is Dylan on that album: a mythic American figure, part flesh-and-

blood man and part American tall tale.

Finally, Lanois helmed Willie Nelson's 1998 album *Teatro* — a more personal reckoning for Nelson. It's a set of songs written long ago, some of them recorded multiple times, but rearranged and resettled in a way that connects them with Nelson's earliest experiences touring nightclubs around Texas. It has the effect of humanizing an artist too often identified by secular relics: the braids, the beard, the bandana, the battered guitar, and the cannabis.

Together, these three albums represent a high point in Lanois' 40-year career, a period when he was taking

> **"You can't ask Bob Dylan to be in the studio for six months. He doesn't come from that world. You'll get him for a month, maybe, and you have to make it work."**
> Daniel Lanois

ideas he had learned while creating ambient music with Brian Eno and stadium-filling rock with U2 and applying them to traditional American music. The results are standouts in each artist's catalog, unique missives about the history and destiny of American country and folk music: how we remember it (woozily, indistinctly, yet crisply, its melodies and rhythms intact) and how it moves into the future (uncertainly, yet undeniably).

The rest of my interview with Lanois, below, chronicles the creation of *Time Out of Mind* and *Teatro*, albums that have an out-of-time quality that marks them as distinctive within each artist's vast catalog. "Out of time and out of mind," says Lanois.

DANIEL LANOIS: When Bob played me the songs that would appear on *Time Out of Mind* early on, I realized he was going to make a blues-based record. The blues had been done so well in America by so many great artists. It's dangerous territory because it's not anything you want to flirt with, or maybe get to a half-baked state with. It's something that you have to command. There was no way that I could command the blues. It's not my territory.

STEPHEN DEUSNER: How did you manage it?

DL: With the help of some technology, I decided to go after a different approach. At the beginning of all this, I met him in a hotel room in New York, and he read me all the lyrics to the songs. I didn't hear a single note. He just read the lyrics and then he said, "What do you think, Daniel? Have we got a record?" I said, "Yeah, Bob, we've got a record."

I got where he was coming from, but he felt that he had the record he wanted by lyric, and it was up to us to frame those lyrics with some kind of significance. He said, "Let me give you a list of records that I like the sound of." They're all really old records. I appreciate that he gave me them to listen to. I knew them already, some of them.

SD: What about those records was inspiring to you?

DL: The records we listened to, they were all *true*. ... They were old records, so they didn't have any of the experimental things from the '60s, when people were fiddling around in studio. They were just raw performances. I thought, "Okay, Bob knows what he's talking about. He wants raw performances, and I wouldn't disagree with him." That's what we went after, even though I brought in some technology.

I took those records to a friend's studio in New York — Tony Mangurian. He's a drummer. In fact, he's one of the drummers on *Teatro*. We put those records on and played along with some of our favorite tracks. We overdubbed some percussion. ... Then we took the blues records out. This is a hip-hop technique, by the way: You put on a

record, play along with it, delete the record, then the toppings might be your friend.

I created about 20 beginnings — loops, you might call them — and I took them to a session with Bob. I figured that if we fall into the bar-band category, if we fall into the category of people trying to play blues in the modern time, then I would pull out these preparations that had a lot of feeling in them. And that did happen. We fell into common blues on a few songs and I got frightened, so I pulled out these preparations and fed them to the drummers as a metronomic source. It was a good three, four, maybe five titles on that record that have that as a rhythmic spine. They don't speed up or slow down. They're very constant. They have that advantage of the groove being this unchanging landscape, almost like a vast desert where the white lines on the highway just stay white forever, and the cacti don't change too much, and the telephone poles are the same. But the storytelling evolves.

SD: It does have that steadiness of tempo. There are a lot of strange grooves on that record.

DL: The grooves are very unusual, even though they're blues grooves. We had the advantage of having a great Southern drummer with us, the great Brian Blade. The Southern drummers have that hi-hat feel, [which] I love. I invited Brian to be involved for that reason: If we're going to mess with the blues, I want a man from the South. And not only from the South, but a man who learned to play with singers in church. Brian's dad is a singing pastor. I thought this music had something sacred about it, so to have not only a musician of his caliber but a church man on board was very comforting.

We also had Jim Keltner, who had worked with Bob many times before. He's very inventive. Brian laid down the grooves, and Jim did some pretty interesting ... toppings, let's call them. We picked up a little bit of a symphonic tonality by having Jim there. And Jim Dickinson. It was Bob's idea to invite him. I didn't know much about Jim, but he was a monster. Sweet man: a monster on the keyboard with a golden heart. He was able to bring a kind of spookiness to a lot of tracks. And we had Augie Meyers, who is an organ player from Texas. It's a very specific thing he does, these little stabbing chords through a Fender Super Reverb.

We had quite a motley crew of players ... [but] it all added up to this new dimension of Americana. It unfolded right in front of my eyes.

I had to give them all a good talking-to at one point, because especially the guitar players were noodling around too much for my taste. I told them, "I don't want any noodling. This is not riff time. It's not time to be flamboyant with your playing. Just think of yourself as something in the landscape that never changes. You're just one of the telephone poles, or one of the wires, or one of the trees. You never change. You're constant. The only thing that changes is the storytelling."

SD: That gives a song like "Dirt Road Blues" a sense of traveling along a path, especially where it descends into these arrhythmic guitars grinding against each other and then comes out of that and back into the groove.

DL: That was a curious journey, because I failed on that one. I tried to cut that song from scratch, and Bob didn't like it. He preferred his demo. He had a cassette he'd done in a rehearsal room, and believe it or not, we took that cassette and dropped it from the multi-track, and everybody played on top of it. It just had a little vibe that he liked, and I couldn't disagree with him. I didn't manage to succeed. I couldn't do better.

SD: "Success" is a word that comes up a lot in your memoir, *Soul Mining*. To measure something as a complete success or a complete failure, with nothing in between, seems pretty intense.

DL: It's a delicate process. You only get so much of someone's time. You can't ask Bob Dylan to be in the studio for six months. He doesn't come from that world. You'll get him for a month, maybe, and you have to make it work. And you have to maintain a level of respect. That's a guy who's made a lot of great records, but had done his best work prior to my working with him a few years before [on 1989's *Oh Mercy*]. I didn't want just a medium record. I wanted to make a classic. Whether I like it or not, that's how I'm good. But then it can hurt me. Sometimes it can hurt other people.

We started the record at my place in Oxnard, California. It's a striking locale, this old, closed-down Mexican cinema that I got going again. That became my shop for a few years. I had a great 100-year-old Steinway piano that I rebuilt — a roaring piano — and Bob sounded great on it. We cut some demos there and got a sound that I was very excited about. I thought the place really suited Bob because it's out of the way. It's serious, and it's a movie theater. He loves old movie posters, and there were a whole bunch still left in the projection room. Everything seemed to be going great, so it came as a surprise to me when he said, "Let's go to Miami to record."

I was mystified, but I didn't want to disagree with him. Okay, we'll go to Miami. Great place, great people, but the piano wasn't as good and the vibe wasn't what it had been back in the Teatro. My heart sank. It was uncomfortable, but eventually we made it work. These are the hurdles you have to cross making records, and sometimes there's nothing you can do about it.

SD: Was there any temptation to quit the project? Or are you completely committed once you start a record?

DL: No, I never went that far. I didn't think I should back out. Once I make a decision to take something on, I have to finish it. It meant a lot to me to make a go at making a masterpiece for a national treasure like Bob Dylan. I did get the feeling that people before me, record makers who worked with Bob before I did, walked on eggshells around him, and maybe they didn't have the guts to stand their ground and push for more. I'm not saying that this is something I like about myself, but [when] push comes to shove, I'm a scrapper. I'm not going to accept mediocrity in anything. That can come back to hurt me and hurt other people.

SD: It sounds like Willie Nelson's *Teatro* was a very different experience than *Time Out of Mind*. You did all the preparation in your own studio, so all he had to do was get off the tour bus and lay down the vocals.

DL: We agreed to meet in Las Vegas. Emmylou was [going] to sing along with him, so she met us in Vegas as well, and we took the bus from Vegas to the Teatro in Oxnard. I had an idea what we were going to do, but I didn't have a full idea. When I talked to Willie, I said, "What was it like when you were a kid? When you were getting started?" He said, "Well, we were just a dance band. We played weekends, and we had to be a good dance band." I asked him, "What kind of songs did you play?" "Well, there was one called 'Lonely Nights.'" He played that one for me, a couple of others, and they

were all quite rhythmic. I decided that it would be nice to capture that dancehall feeling. That's what made me think of getting those two drummers: Victor Indrizzo, a great drummer in L.A., and Tony Mangurian. Tony's a left-handed drummer, and Victor's a right, so we were able to build one big kit for the two of them.

We played up this whole smoking thing, Cuban cigars and all that, so they had a big ashtray with a swag lamp over them. It was quite sweet because the two guys were, by proximity, very close. Rhythmically it was pretty on. I didn't want to have a bass player because I didn't want anybody to make mistakes. [I] can't have a bass player make a mistake, [that] just fucks everything up. I overdubbed the bass afterwards. I became Willie Nelson's bandleader and bass player for a while, and was playing at Farm Aid.

I played bass on half of Dylan's *Oh Mercy*. To have knowledge of the material was something that was important in the making of those records. By the time we got to Miami with Dylan, I really had an understanding of the structure of the songs, and so I able to really warm up the band prior to Bob's arrival. The same thing happened with Willie. I had the band very lubricated by the time Willie was ready. The Teatro had a nice big parking lot, and Willie had his bus out there. He'd wait for me to come up and fetch him from the bus. He'd come in and

we'd do one, two, maybe three takes, but probably just one or two. We had set up the place so he and Emmy were on a riser, and it really felt like a little club. We really got a nice vibe going. I think Willie really appreciated that people didn't have to wear headphones. The drummers wore headphones, but nobody else.

It had a good vibe like a Cuban nightclub. Willie would get a good take and then go back to his bus. I'd do a bass part, then we'd move on to the next song. I'd teach that song to the band, and when they felt they had it down pretty good, I'd go to the bus and fetch Willie again and bring him in. It happened pretty quick. He loved that because he didn't get studio fatigue [while] waiting in the green room or playing pinball somewhere. He was able to go to his bus. Again, the place had a small-town feeling, and we were in pretty good with the cops. I have a friend on the police force there, so they turned a blind eye to some of the, um, stuff that might have been happening on Willie's bus. [These are] things you've got to do.

SD: That strategy of only bringing him in for the vocal takes seems like it would encourage a lot of spontaneity in his performances.

DL: Yeah, there's nothing like those fresh takes. You play a song too many times, you start thinking of ways of improving it, [and] you lose that first instinct to do things in a thoughtless manner. Thinking too much is the enemy of music; "thoughtless" can apply in a very positive situation. ... You know how people always sound good in their kitchens? Then they go in the studio, "Oh, jeez. The drum pedal's squeaking, and my guitar's got rattle." Things you never hear at home, you hear in the studio. Well, we didn't have those problems because it felt like home. You get that communication where you can see people's lips moving, all the little

nuance, a twinkle in the eye, a side glance. Those little things go a long way. If you start putting people in booths with headphones on, then you lose that communication system.

... I don't think I could make those records now because I live in a different time of my life. Back then I believed in those projects so much, and

it meant so much to me to help those artists create classics to live by. I don't like to do disposable things. Life's too short. I still stand by those values now. We just made the music that we felt was the most beautiful, and would elevate listeners and cause them to have thoughts of their own. And isn't that the job of art? ∎

she come by it natural

Part Four:

Through philanthropy and frank talk, Dolly Parton cements her icon status

This concludes the four-part series on Dolly Parton by our No Depression Writing Fellow, Sarah Smarsh.

By Sarah Smarsh

During the 2017 Emmy Awards, Dolly Parton reunited with *9 to 5* co-stars Jane Fonda and Lily Tomlin to present an award during the live broadcast. All three were nominated for Emmys themselves — Fonda and Tomlin for acting in the Netflix comedy series *Grace and Frankie*, in which they play upper-class friends living beachside in southern California, and Parton for producing the 2016 television movie *Christmas of Many Colors*, in which she plays an Appalachian prostitute.

Onstage with Parton and Tomlin, Fonda pointed out their role as feminist elders.

"Back in 1980, in [*9 to 5*], we refused to be controlled by a sexist, egotistical, lying, hypocritical bigot," Fonda said.

Tomlin added, to cheers, making an obvious reference to the sitting president, "In 2017, we still refuse to be controlled by a sexist, hypocritical, lying, egotistical bigot."

In just those two lines, Fonda and Tomlin told the world something about gender. But Parton knew it might be more effective to *show* it. Standing between her two friends, Parton referenced a season-two storyline from their series: "I'm just hoping that I'm going to get one of those *Grace and Frankie* vibrators in my swag bag tonight."

Hers was the least directly political comment of the three. It was also the one most assured to piss off a man like Donald Trump — in whose eyes women exist for his pleasure, diminish in value as they age, and need a man in order to get sexual pleasure. A 71-year-old woman having the nerve to fantasize about a sex toy on national television after the president's name was invoked? If you wonder whether that was intentional, you might rewatch *9 to 5*, in which Parton's character shoves a pistol in the face of a male boss who has a habit of grabbing her and then bragging about it.

The stars of that feminist film found themselves addressing the past in the present, the horrifying office boss made leader of the world. In order to be effective, such a task requires finesse. Who better than Parton for the job? After all, she has spent 50 years fighting the systemic sexism of Nashville.

Like the entire nation, for which conservativism now shapes law and dominates the White House, the country music industry is suffering a swing backwards, against gains women made in the '60s, '70s, and '80s. During the first half of 2016, songs by female artists accounted for less than 10 percent of country radio plays, according to *Forbes* magazine. In that same time, only five female artists appeared on *Billboard's* Top 30 Country Airplay charts.

The previous year, an influential country-radio consultant, Keith Hill, explained why stations keep their rotations overwhelmingly male. Hill told *Country Aircheck*, "If you want to make ratings in country radio, take females out." Women, he said, were "just not the lettuce in our salad. The lettuce is Luke Bryan, Blake Shelton, Keith Urban, and artists like that. The tomatoes of our salad are the females."

The comment sparked an overdue controversy about an old problem, and female artists expressed their displeasure. Martina McBride sold "tomato" shirts to raise money for her charity; Jennifer Nettles tweeted that the moment was a "big old vagina-shaped opportunity."

Men and women alike on the music-business side defended Hill's comment with claims about numbers and data: There aren't enough good female records, female songs don't test as well, even female listeners prefer male singers when you crunch the numbers. But it wasn't always this way — whatever factors are behind such data, they say more about prevailing cultural attitudes of the moment than about the quality of women's music.

The last time Dolly Parton had a solo number-one hit, "Why'd You Come in Here Looking Like That" in 1989, female artists were riding high in the industry, making way for the halcyon 1990s of Reba, Faith, and Shania. But a recent Stanford University study found that, despite record labels continuing to introduce new women artists, women have fallen down the charts since the turn of the millennium.

Parton once attributed her own absence from the charts to the fact that she is now an artist of a certain age.

"When the new country came along, any artist over 35 was thought to be a has-been," she told *Rolling Stone* in 2003. "And, Lord, I've been around for so long that people looked at me like a legend. But I wasn't near done. I felt like I was better than I ever was. I feel like I'm just now seasoned enough to know how to be in this business. And I thought, 'Well, hell, I'm not going down with the rest of them old farts. I'm gonna find some new ways of doing it.' And that's exactly what I did."

Indeed, Parton had founded her own record label in 1993, at age 48, and went about doing things however she wanted. "I thought, 'Well, now I can record the stuff I really want to,' and I don't have 14 managers and record executives saying, 'Oh, you gotta be more commercial, you gotta be more pop.' I thought, 'I don't care if I write [a song that is] six or seven minutes long — I'm gonna tell the story.' I'm not gonna think, 'Oh, I have to cut this down to fit the radio.' If they play it on the radio, fine. Doubt if they would, and don't care anymore."

Perhaps it is no coincidence that women lost footing in popular country music amid the larger backlash against feminist gains. Today's young female singer-songwriters who follow in Parton's footsteps — old twang, modern ideas, gothic country themes, spiritual vulnerability — get good reviews, sell records, and sell out shows whether they're underplayed on country radio or not. But such artists — like superstar Miranda Lambert, rising sensation Kacey Musgraves, and indie favorite Valerie June — are working in an industry currently betting against them. One doubts a young Dolly Parton, with her dark songs about poor country women knocked up and abandoned by wayward men, would have much chance at making it in Nashville today.

Keeping It Real

Parton's late-career decisions have revealed a commitment to authenticity over hit-making. Since going rogue with her own label in the early '90s, Parton has released more than a dozen solo albums of new material. Three of those, around the turn of the millennium — just as slick pop country from acts like Keith Urban

"When the new country came along, any artist over 35 was thought to be a has-been. ... And I thought, 'Well, hell, I'm not going down with the rest of the them old farts. I'm gonna find some new ways of doing it.'" - Dolly Parton

and Rascal Flatts was taking over the airwaves — were thoroughly bluegrass, including a 2001 cover of Collective Soul's "Shine" that won her a Grammy.

The music from the first half of her career remains her signature, and is now being discovered by a generation born after Parton disappeared from country radio. Where Parton was a sweet country singer to Baby Boomers and a crossover Hollywood star to Generation X, she is to millennials a spiritual godmother, her big-haired 1970s likeness on novelty-store shelves on devotional candles representing feminine power. Whether she has another groundbreaking hit or not, her entire life is now understood to have broken ground — for female artists, for poor girls with dreams, for women who would like to be bosses without hiding their breasts. This evolution was a slow unfolding over the course of a lifetime, but if one had to pinpoint a moment when Parton came to terms with her own living legend status, it might be England's Glastonbury Festival in 2014.

After having no manager for 17 years, in the early 2000s Parton hired Nashville manager Danny Nozell to help organize a tour. Nozell ended up crafting a plan to market her work to a younger generation around the world. She sold out a tour in Europe in 2007, an arena tour in 2008, and two Australian tours. But Parton said no to booking requests from Glastonbury — a decidedly rock-and-roll gathering of some 200,000 people — from 2006 to 2013. Her fervent fan base has been global for decades, but she worried the rock-and-roll festival wouldn't be a good fit, according to a 2014 interview with *The Guardian*.

When she finally took the leap in 2014 as a Glastonbury headliner, not even Parton understood what was about to happen: An estimated 180,000 people gathered to see her — the biggest crowd in Glastonbury history. Another 2.6 million watched live on the BBC, the network's largest audience for its festival coverage.

Glastonbury was a long way from the East Tennessee farm where, as a child, Parton made a mock microphone from a tin can and stick and sang for the hogs. She had left that farm 50 years prior and made sure to honor those origins in front of the huge international crowd. She wrote a song called "Mud" just for the infamously muddy festival, and told the chanting crowd where she'd done her research. "I grew up on a farm," Parton said, "so this mud ain't nothin' new to me." It's a line that might make a fine country song about Parton's relationship to sexism in Nashville.

Part of her successful strategy for connecting with young fans in recent years has been to collaborate with much younger artists. On pop star Kesha's most recent album, out last August, Parton sings a duet of her own number-one hit from 1980, "Old Flames (Can't Hold a Candle to You)," which Kesha's mother, Pebe Sebert, wrote. Earlier this year, Parton covered Brandi Carlile's signature song, "The Story," for an album benefiting a nonprofit that aids refugee children. And she won a 2017 Grammy for Best Country Duo/Group Performance for her "Jolene" recording remixed by young a capella group Pentatonix.

Parton has long shown up for her millennial goddaughter, Miley Cyrus — making a cameo on her Disney TV show, bringing her onstage, singing with her on *The Voice* — perhaps to the benefit of both. A journalist friend of mine once told me that he had been watching the World Cup at a bar in Venezuela with Hugo Chávez when Chávez's daughter told him that she and her friend loved the "new Miley Cyrus song" about a woman named Jolene. He showed them a video of the Parton original on his phone, and they were dazzled.

Much of the new fandom might not be able to name more than five Parton songs, but Parton's presence is so multifaceted that they will have plenty of opportunity to learn more. Yes, there is her ubiquitous presence in pop culture: Her songs have been recorded by superstars as divergent as Nancy Sinatra and Patti Smith, Kitty Wells and Whitney Houston. Some of her movies, most notably *9 to 5* and *Steel Magnolias*, are now considered classics. But late-career Parton is now seen as much more: a business mogul, a philanthropic juggernaut, an auspiciously progressive voice in conservative spaces.

In her home county in Tennessee, her amusement park Dollywood and other Parton attractions annually spur more than a billion dollars in economic impact for the state. Her literacy project, Imagination Library, has given more than 80 million books to more than one million children around the world, according to the foundation. Her outspoken progressivism regarding gay and transgender rights, gender parity, and other issues have pushed country music to evolve, while her open Christian faith and homespun vernacular have made her a bridge between crossover fans and the poor, rural South.

During the fall 2017 semester, the University of Tennessee offered a history course that used Parton's life story to examine Appalachia in the 20th century, from child-labor laws to today's economic struggles. There is a rose named after her; there is a film (the 2015 indie *Seeking Dolly Parton*) named after the rose. Parton is now to country music what Oprah Winfrey is to media — a natural talent who, simply by being herself, transcended an industry to transform society.

Part of the transformation she helmed was women's progress in country music. Yes, Nashville is still rooted in patriarchy, but some of the interview questions she got in years past would cause a feminist Twitter riot today. In cultural chatter, there is a palpable new reverence for Parton as a multidimensional human being.

Perhaps due to her looks and persona — at once exaggerated gender performance and sincere, unapologetic feminine sexuality — until recent years Parton had not received the same gravitas that music journalists or Hollywood long ago afforded, say, Loretta Lynn, whose life was mined for the Oscar-winning biopic *Coal Miners' Daughter* and whose music spurred the unironic admiration and collaboration of indie darling Jack White. But seen in the light of the 21st century, with woke young female fans and greater gender parity in the media that sets the narratives about her, Parton's iconography finally shifts from coveted object to the divine feminine — a sassy priestess in high heels.

Giving Back

Parton has said that one of her greatest professional joys is her relationship to children who receive free books through her Imagination Library, which she founded in 1995. Innocent of her celebrity, those kids call her "the book lady," she told *PBS NewsHour* in 2013. They receive a free book in the mail from every month from birth until age five.

"Children have always responded to me because I have that cartoon-character look," Parton told *Time* magazine in 2009, when she released her own children's book titled *I Am a Rainbow*. "I'm overexaggerated and my voice is small and my name is Dolly and I'm kind of like a Mother Goose character."

Parton's father, Lee, inspired her concern for literacy. A tobacco farmer and construction worker born in 1921, he never had the opportunity to learn to read. That background, the bedrock of Parton's famous climb from poverty, might be why the first book each child in the program receives is *The Little Engine That Could* — the lessons of which are vintage Dolly. The book has been performed as a live show at Dollywood's Imagination Playhouse, which brings many of the program's selections to life.

Imagination Library, often facilitated by county libraries, requires no income documentation or other hoop-jumping — just a quick form with an address and the child's birth date to confirm age eligibility. This decision by the umbrella Dollywood Foundation indicates someone involved knows what it's like to be a child in need.

Since everyone is eligible, the neediest children can benefit without feeling ashamed of being recipients of a poor-people's program.

Parton's relief funds for victims of last year's Smoky Mountain wildfires were, similarly, low on red tape. Affected families, whether homeowners or renters, provided proof of address to receive $1,000 per month for six months from the Dollywood Foundation, with few questions asked. At the end of that period, last May, Parton visited some of the 900 families who had received assistance to make an announcement, and the *Tennessean* shared video of an exchange with one beneficiary.

"I'm gonna give you an additional five thousand dollars," Parton said, making the total gift $11,000 for each household.

"An additional — " a surprised older man in a University of Tennessee ball cap said.

"That's like a bonus that you didn't know you were gettin'," Parton said, slapping him on the shoulder.

"God bless you for doin' this for us," he said in a serious tone. "For all these people."

"It's the least I can do," Parton said. "I'm a Smoky Mountain girl. I mean, this is home. Charity begins at home, right?"

A white-haired woman sitting next to the man interjected. "Nobody but you would be so kind and generous," she said, starting to cry. Parton, standing, wiped tears from the woman's face.

"I'm sure nearly anybody up here would do that," Parton said. "These are good people."

"You're our people," the man replied, nodding. "Whether we're your people or not, you're our people."

"You *are* my people," Parton said, and she wasn't pandering. To address the long-term needs of those who lost their homes and more, she gave $3 million to establish the Mountain Tough fund, through which social workers can secure medication for fire-related health problems, rides to work, and more for low-income fire victims.

I often see surprised reactions to Parton's philanthropy, from the millions of books mailed to children to the millions of dollars raised for fire victims, from the decades of high school scholarships to Tennessee high school seniors to the health care foundation she established in 1983 and named for the beloved country doctor who delivered her. Other famous people are as generous

as she is, one imagines. But I've never seen people so shocked upon learning about celebrity philanthropy as those who learn about Parton's.

Perhaps this is because, for most of her giving over the years, there has been no photo op or press release — just a quiet check and Parton's name on a board of directors. Imagination Library, in particular, kept a low profile for nearly 30 years, which must have been Parton's preference at the time. But children's author Robert Munsch, featured in a 2009 documentary about Parton's book program, got down to the real matter of why her good heart comes as such a revelation.

"I thought of Dolly Parton as this singer with the really big boobs who was in the movies with, like, the really big boobs," Munsch said. "I didn't really have much of an idea."

Big Business

People might not have much of an idea about the extent of Parton's business empire, either. In addition to her music, books, movies, TV shows, and even restaurant forays over the years, in 1986 she co-founded Sandollar Productions with her legendary manager Sandy Gallin. The company's successes range from blockbuster hits like the 1991 comedy *Father of the Bride* and the television series *Buffy the Vampire Slayer* to cultural milestones like *Stories from the Quilt*, the 1989 AIDS film that won the Academy Award for best documentary.

Surpassing even blockbuster Hollywood success, in financial terms, is Parton's enduring Dollywood, an amusement park in Pigeon Forge, Tennessee, that draws three million visitors to the area every year. The park, which opened in the 1980s after Parton listened to her instincts rather than to the financial advisers who pooh-poohed her vision, is rooted in Parton's native place and class.

Writer Keith Bellows, who lived in East Tennessee for 15 years, vouched for the attraction's deep connection to the local people in a story for *National Geographic Traveler* in 2009.

"I was charmed by [Dolly's] practice of populating the park with genuine Appalachian craftspeople, musicians, artists," Bellows wrote. "That was rare back then — but she's always been a trendsetter."

Parton told Bellows that decision

was foundational to the business: "I wanted people working there who were connected with the land and the local culture. They made it real, not phony. It made me feel comfortable. And I guess I thought it would make the visitors feel that way, too."

The place was previously a Silver Dollar City location, modeled on a park in Branson, Missouri, with a rural Ozarks theme. Parton came on board in 1986, adding her own stamp and her name. Parton's presence is everywhere, including the Dolly museum and a replica of the house she grew up in.

While many amusement parks create an atmosphere of fantasy intended to sweep visitors into another place full of magical characters, Parton's impulse was to exalt the natural setting and working people that shaped her — keeping it local before local was cool. "I'm keen to maintain the soul of the place," Parton told Bellows. "To celebrate God's beauty — that means go for a nice walk, smell that air, feel the temperature, hold on to the sense of the moment, take a drift on a trail, look deeply into the stream. That means so much more than all the artifice in the world."

Country music scholar Pamela Fox, examining country music autobiographies in the academic journal *American Quarterly* in 1998, pointed out that Dollywood not only celebrates the Smoky Mountains for the rest of the world, but champions that region's poorest people within the context of their own home. "Chiding those critics who dismiss the theme park as a vanity project," Fox wrote, "Parton insists that the business honors 'her people' by employing 'mostly real hillbillies' to showcase mountain culture. At the same time, she planned the park to resemble old-time, small-town carnivals — the ostensible Other of that hardscrabble world."

A cynic might say that, even with good intentions, Parton has exploited that socioeconomic, geographic Other — the rural poor — for her own gain. By employing people of the region, one could argue that Dollywood demands those people make a performance out of their authentic lives, as other cultures and entire races have been commanded to do for more privileged people in exchange for money and survival. But the difference with Dollywood is that Parton was and is of the place.

Her own ideas about her place, her people, and herself are inevitably tied up in the American culture. She jokes about "white trash," a term I refuse to use as a white person who grew up in rural poverty. But that's the difference between directly opposing degradation and seizing its means — the latter being Parton's preferred method. To fight the dehumanization of the rural poor, Parton got rich, went home, and turned Appalachia into a performance before rich New York developers could. It was not unlike her habit of cracking a joke about the size of her breasts before the male talk-show host has a chance to.

In fact, she went so far as to put her first name on the place — Dollywood, located just a few miles from the very spot where she was born — so there would be no mistake: Parton stands with the people who work there and whose spirits are evoked there for entertainment, not just in the past they share but in the present moment in which she cuts their checks, sends their high schoolers to college, funds a foundation to ensure their health care, and holds a telethon when wildfires take their houses. While wages at the amusement park are standard for that industry — low hourly pay for seasonal hires such as students on summer break — all employees have access to an onsite health care center, and full-time employees of the park receive comprehensive health insurance benefits.

Make no mistake — Parton set out to get rich and enjoy being rich, and that she has done. This year, for the first time, thanks to Dollywood's continued boom and her 2016 tour, she made the *Forbes* list of the world's 100 highest-paid entertainers — at number 71, above Rihanna, Billy Joel, Toby Keith, and Katy Perry. As for how she spends the spoils of wealth, fame, and cultural connections, Parton has said that she and her husband enjoy hitting the road in an RV and getting their meals from fast-food drive-through windows.

"I'm a truck stop girl," she said in the *National Geographic Traveler* story. "Honest. I'm not an act. I go into Cracker Barrel and browse the shelf. Mostly I look for real stuff. My husband and I pull off the road to look at any old antique store. It's 'Dolly is coming' — I blow in there, fly into the room, and get something wonderful that says I've been there. I just love my junk stuff. Wigs are what people think of when they picture

me. But what I really look for is what my Daddy would love."

She also has a taste for real estate, she told *Billboard* in 2014. She owns a residence in Los Angeles and two in Tennessee. One imagines there might be more she doesn't talk about publicly. "It's not to say, 'Hey, look at me,'" she explained. "I'd rather buy property than play the stock market."

That most of her real estate investments are in her native Smokies parallels every other aspect of her career. She could afford to look refined and sophisticated but has held fast to a personal style modeled after her poor-country vision of glamour. She could adapt the way she speaks in the company of higher classes but keeps on saying "ain't." She could sing and speak about her world travels and decades of rarefied experiences but keeps talking about the poor folks what brung her. As Jancee Dunn wrote for *Rolling Stone* in 2003, "Many people who are raised in near-poverty try to distance themselves from their upbringing, but not Parton, whose ticket out turned into a round-trip."

That round-trip is not just in spirit but in the flesh. Parton is known to be physically present at the park, whether for an event or to shop in her own stores. "I love Dollywood, because I love to go shopping up there in the stores," she told Dunn. "I think, 'Oh, good, I don't have to pay for this.' I'm taking advantage of myself."

Hits and Misses

However thoughtful and self-aware, Parton's career and empire is not impeccable. One truly problematic rhinestone in Parton's business crown is Dixie Stampede, a dinner-theater experience that will celebrate its 30th year in 2018.

Held in a 35,000-square-foot rodeo arena that seats more than a thousand people, the daily show features horse-riding stunts like barrel racing and musical productions while visitors eat chicken with their fingers. While Parton's message is usually a class-conscious argument for love and acceptance, Dixie Stampede is a squarely patriotic event with a lot of red, white, and blue and a heavy dose of white-washed nostalgia for the Antebellum South. The show's overarching theme is the Civil War, and patrons are asked to choose which side they'll cheer for, North or South.

Locations include Pigeon Forge, home of Dollywood and her nearby water park, and a second spot in Branson, Missouri. Another operated for 18 years in Myrtle Beach, S.C., until Parton spent $11 million to transform it into a pirate-themed dinner-theater attraction in 2010. A shorter-lived location opened near Disney World in Florida in 2003 and closed five years later.

In 2015, the remaining Tennessee and Missouri locations underwent a $2.5 million update, including new music and special effects. According to Parton's website, by that point more than 20 million people had visited.

I went to the Branson location with my family years before that update, and found the operation to be far removed from Parton in both spirit and actual presence. A recording of Parton's voice plays multiple times over the show, carefully suggesting that she herself might appear, which I found maddening and insulting to visitors' intelligence.

As for the show itself, I grew up going to rodeos and love a good barrel race as much as the next gal. But when I waited in line at Dixie Stampede, I was in college, learning about my home state Kansas' pivotal role in sparking the Civil War by declaring itself a free state. During that period, abolitionist blood was shed at the Missouri border, and Kansas has a strained relationship with Missouri and Confederacy glorification to this day. Perhaps that is why, even as a relatively ignorant and privilege-oblivious young white woman, I wasn't impressed with a storyline that sanitizes the Civil War as cheesy entertainment and presents the Union and Confederacy as two equal sides.

Last August, after the renovation, *Slate* culture writer Aisha Harris penned an overdue critique of Dixie Stampede, calling it a "lily-white kitsch extravaganza that play-acts the Civil War but never once mentions slavery." The Confederate flag doesn't make an appearance to represent the South, but a gray flag evokes that army's uniform color. The show ultimately wraps with a message that we're all part of one United States of America.

Attending two 2017 performances to research her piece, Harris noted the presence of people of color among the crowd, employees, and performers. As a black woman, she said she felt uncomfortable watching such a delusional spectacle unfold.

"Standing in front of the box office were two young women who looked like the cast of *The Beguiled,* or Southern belles from *Gone with the Wind*, greeting patrons as they made their way into the building," Harris wrote. "Once inside and past the ticket scanners, you were forced to take a group photo in one of several partitioned quarters in front of a green backdrop. Rather than immortalizing this unwanted re-enactment in the form of a $30 souvenir, I asked not to have my picture taken and hurried past while trying to blend in with the family in front of me."

Harris, who shared that she was a Parton fan, pointed out that this unfortunate piece of Parton's world exemplified the same sort of denial that allows white people to defend Confederate monuments or to see white-supremacist rallies and anti-racism protesters as moral equivalents.

"Dolly's Dixie Stampede has been a success not just because people love Dolly Parton, but because the South has always been afforded the chance to rewrite its own history — not just through its own efforts, but through the rest of the country turning a blind eye," Harris wrote. "Even though the South is built upon the foundation of slavery, a campy show produced by a well-meaning country superstar can make-believe it's not."

A few weeks after her story ran, Harris reported for *Slate* that she had reached out for a response from Dixie Stampede and been told via email that they would "evaluate the information provided by Ms. Harris in her Slate.com article in regard to our Pigeon Forge and Branson operations."

While that initial response could be described as lacking, Harris generously shared her hope that the business might make real changes. "As an admirer of Parton's other work in movies and music," she wrote, "and as someone who believes that it matters how honestly we tell our nation's history, it's nice to hear that my review might inspire the show's creators to reconsider its framing and presentation."

This white-washing of history is particularly confounding when one considers that, over the decades, Parton has taken bold stands for the LGBTQ community, for women, and for the poor. Her statement on all the rest, from race to political affiliation, has remained a message of love in general terms. But

now, Parton's late-career power and presence happens to coincide with a fractious moment in America. What will she do with it?

She referenced the volatile state of the country onstage during her 2016 tour, commenting on the madness of that year's divisive presidential election and race-related police shootings and unrest. Then she performed a moving handful of folk songs that were popular the last time our culture was at such a boiling point — the beginning of her career, the fraught 1960s.

Glittering in rhinestones and holding forth with the strong voice from her diaphragm that I've always preferred to the soft, girly voice she affects for some of her hits, she sang "If I Had a Hammer" and other counterculture classics while her unplugged musicians joined her with an upright bass, guitar, and tambourine. Much of the crowd sang along, some in tears during that difficult year. It was apparent that Parton is a singer, yes, but foremost a healer who understands when people are hurting.

Nip It, Tuck It, Suck It

In society's eyes, the aging of a beloved celebrity artist often requires another kind of moral reckoning — as culture evolves, does that person's ethics stand the test of time? Bill Cosby's alleged serial rapes went unchecked amid the sexist culture of his younger days but are the stuff of career ruin today. Meanwhile, sentiment toward Jane Fonda's Vietnam War protest, for which she was vilified for decades, has softened as prevailing attitudes toward the US's involvement there are more critical.

For women, however, there is another gauntlet in the maturation process — how their face and body look as they age. Parton has famously had a tremendous amount of plastic surgery and makes no bones about it. She believes she has an image to maintain and seems to share a preference for the vitality a young form represents. "I have done it and will do it again when something in my mirror doesn't look to me like it belongs on Dolly Parton," she wrote in in her 1994 autobiography. "I feel it is my duty to myself and my public. My spirit is too beautiful and alive to live in some dilapidated old body if it doesn't have to."

Country music scholar Pamela Fox, in her 1988 *American Quarterly* article, suggested that Parton's impoverished upbringing made her comfortable with a sense of detachment from her own body, which had been previously put to use for work, whether slopping hogs or squeezed into a costume.

In the process of surgical reconstruction, Fox wrote, " 'Dolly Parton' becomes a separate, almost reified persona which her body literally creates. ... Parton understands that gender is performance: achieving the right hair color, conforming to a seemingly impossible hour-glass bodily ideal. But it is a performance she can pull off with astounding success. ... She exchanges the class-based objectification of her past for a gender-based one in the present. The Dolly character represents the literal embodiment of her own personal 'dream.' "

To that end, a decision that causes some feminists to shake their heads and lament what a pity it is that Parton has gone to such surgical lengths indeed seems to represent, for Parton, a success as outsized as her wig. In 2004, she told CBS, "I always said, if I see something sagging, bagging, and dragging, I'm going to nip it, tuck it, and suck it. Whatever needs to be done. I mean, it's like I look at myself like a show horse, or

a show dog. ... I've always had nice boobs. I always had a nice body when I was little, but when I lost all that weight, I had them pumped up, and fixed up. They just stand up there like brave little soldiers now. They're real big, they're real expensive, and they're really mine now."

Thus, Parton's sense of ownership about her breasts, her body, and decisions about them is a defiant act in a culture that managed to obsess over her breasts so thoroughly that the first cloned mammal, a sheep in 1996, was named after her.

Further, Parton's response to double standards about male and female bodies is not to embrace her own aging but, rather, chastise men for theirs. During a 2003 taping of CMT's "Crossroads" series with Melissa Etheridge, Parton told the familiar lore about her song "Jolene" — a pretty bank employee caught her husband's eye early in their marriage, and Parton's song begged her not to take him.

"I look at him now," she joked between songs, next to Etheridge, "[and] I think about hiding his Viagra and saying, 'Go get him.' "

Later in the set, the pair performed another song about jealousy, Etheridge's early-career rock tune "Bring Me

Some Water." Parton sang the lyrics with passion and changed the verb "whispering" to something wilder: "Tell me how will I ever be the same / When I know that woman is somewhere screaming your name." As the song wound down, though, Parton's tone suddenly changed from tortured to commanding, and she decided to invent another character, for her own amusement. "Hey, little water boy," Parton said, unsmiling, her hand on her hip. "Bring the bucket around." Etheridge cracked up.

As for men her age, Parton isn't cutting them any slack. During a 2013 *Good Morning America* interview next to Parton, her longtime friend and duet partner Kenny Rogers referred to his own famously altered face and how Parton has chided him for it. "When [the media] got on that whole plastic surgery thing, that was a bit painful even though it was true," Rogers said. "Dolly used to say, 'Look, ol' Kenny's been to Jiffy Suck again.' "

Sitting next to him, Parton took his chin in her hand and examined his face while he tried to pull away. "I think he's really grown into his face-lift now, don't you?" she said and laughed. "He looks great."

The greater revelation about gender and country music specifically — and gender and society in general — isn't Parton and Rogers' respective relationships to physically aging but the time it took each of them to receive due honors as industry greats. The second recipient of the Country Music Awards' Willie Nelson Lifetime Achievement Award, a year after Nelson himself received it in 2012, was Rogers, whose career has been illustrious but pales next to Parton's in both artistry and cultural impact.

Parton has written and published hundreds of songs and is celebrated by critics and fans alike as a creative genius. In 2005, the National Endowment for the Arts awarded her the country's highest honor for contribution to creative fields, the National Medal of the Arts, in a White House ceremony. Rogers, meanwhile, rose to fame as a good-looking guy who happily showed up in the studio to lend his smooth voice to someone else's words.

"I take great pride in not writing hits," Rogers told NPR when his autobiography, *Luck or Something Like It*, was released in 2012. "I write from time to time, but I

think great writers have a need to write, and I don't really have that need. I can write if someone sits me down and says, 'Hey let's write a song about this.'"

Of course, plenty of music legends don't write their own songs, and Rogers' career achievements are immense, but his career benefited directly from Parton's. As Rogers recalled on *Good Morning America*, he was recording "Islands in the Stream" solo with lackluster results when producer Barry Gibb mused that they needed Parton to "make it pop." Now the song is one of the bestselling duets of all time and a pop-culture mainstay. Parton didn't write that one, but her presence next to him in the studio and onstage is what ensured his legacy.

"There's no question it's kind of the crown to everything," he added on GMA. "To have done the song with her and have it be accepted so highly worldwide. No matter where I go, the one thing they always ask for is 'Islands in the Stream.'"

Despite all this, it was Rogers, not Parton, who got the Lifetime Achievement award for country music first — suggesting that the "luck" in his book title might have more than a little to do with being a man.

The next year, the award went to Johnny Cash, posthumously. Then, in 2015, when Parton was the first female and fourth performer to receive the award, she suffered the indignity of being cut off when she'd barely begun her acceptance speech. During the presentation honoring her, *9 to 5* costar and friend Lily Tomlin spoke before Jennifer Nettles, Pentatonix, Reba McEntire, Kacey Musgraves, Carrie Underwood, and Martina McBride each sang Parton's hits. By the time Parton finally took the stage, one minute into her speech, producers promptly cued her to wrap it up.

"They asked me to hurry it up. They said that they're behind," she told the audience. "But we're talking about a lifetime here." She wrapped up at the two-minute mark with a big smile, saying, "I had a big speech but they won't let me give it." Then Sharon Stone slowly sauntered across the stage and presented Best Male Artist to Chris Stapleton, who was embarrassed. "If Dolly's still back there," he said, "I'd give her my time." But the show moved on.

The reaction on Twitter from across the cultural and political spectrum was swift.

"Really #CMAawards50 you couldn't let the legendary @DollyParton give her speech for a lifetime of country music? No bueno," film critic Carla Renata tweeted.

Conservative commentator Meghan McCain didn't mince words: "Who in the holy hell wouldn't let @DollyParton finish her speech for her lifetime achievement award?!?!"

And New York drag queen Darienne Lake tweeted, "My biggest devastation of the night, cutting @DollyParton's speech short. Everyone should be fired at the #CMAawards50. EVERYONE!"

Later in the evening, meanwhile, Entertainer of the Year Garth Brooks got plenty of time to speak. I'm not suggesting there was some big conspiracy to cut Parton short and give the time to male performers and award winners. But, as the radio programming consultant's "tomato" comment revealed, show business is a world of calculations informed by gender. And that night at the CMAs — if only in a hasty moment subconsciously informed by culture and implicit bias — someone decided that Parton's speech was worth less than a series of moments starring men.

So Much Substance

A woman's voice, whether on the radio, onstage, or, say, in the 2016 presidential race, will be celebrated but only so far. The airplay will be minimized. The speech will be cut short. The candidate may be beloved by some, while others yell, "Lock her up."

Parton, surely among the least divisive figures in pop culture, receives little in the way of antagonism. But as a female boss, she too faces the sexist onus of likability. In 2014, *Billboard* asked her, "As a Southern woman, how do you speak your mind and take care of business but remain likable?"

Parton didn't seem to be losing any sleep over the issue. "I'm open and I'm honest," she replied. "I don't dillydally. If there's something going on, I just say it. Sometimes if I get mad, I'll throw out a few cuss words just to prove my point. I've often said I don't lose my temper as much as I use it. I don't do either unless I have to because I love peace and harmony, but when you step in my territory, I will call you on it. People say, 'Oh, you just always seem so happy.' Well, that's the Botox."

The glass ceiling that made lifelong public servant Hillary Clinton lose an election to perhaps the most morally bankrupt idiot to ever seek office is the same one that made Dolly Parton answer more questions about her measurements than her songwriting over the decades. The two women took very different feminist tacks, of course. But, at almost exactly the same age, they share an experience — to break through, toward an equality that they themselves will never enjoy.

Who, then, will follow in Parton's footsteps and reap the benefits of her struggles? While plenty of young female roots-music artists owe Parton a debt and count her as an influence, only a boldly constructed character could truly carry her mantle.

A couple years ago, VH1 theorized that character might be hip-hop artist Nicki Minaj. Media critic Jade Davis expanded on the theory, citing "the two artists' big hair, generous physical assets, curve-enhancing sartorial habits, and keen business sense."

They're also both musicians in lowbrow, male-dominated genres. They both embrace being objects in the spaces where they're allowed to exist. Both serve the gendered fantasies of their respective social milieus. Parton lovingly refers to herself as the "backwoods Barbie." Similarly, Minaj's longest-running and most famous stage [persona] is the Harajuku Barbie. In many ways, the two inhabit a Barbie-like existence. They are pop stars, businesswomen, sex symbols of ridiculous proportions.

But even though they draw inspiration from the fakest woman on the planet, they keep it realer than anyone. They don't need to stand in front of glowing "FEMINIST" signs or writhe around with lubricant on their bodies. They live, breathe, and perform what everyone else tries so hard to convey: I own myself.

Indeed, Parton represents a place, culture, and generation for which the term "feminism" is more suspicious than a woman embodying its meaning. She thus helped pioneer the sort of feminism on display in contemporary pop music — serving up T&A on your own terms, subverting objectification by having a damn good time with it — but perhaps not while speaking the same language as progressive America. While appearing on CNN in 2015, a caller asked Parton if she would describe herself as a feminist.

"Oh, I'm a — I'm a female and I

believe that everybody should definitely have their rights," she said. "I don't care if you're black, white, straight, gay, women, men, whatever. I think everybody that has something to offer should be allowed to give it and be paid for it. But, no, I don't consider myself a feminist, not in the term that some people do, because I — I just think we all should be treated with respect."

Her answer might break your heart if, like me, you speak the language of a college-educated activist. But I speak another language, too — poor country — and can attest that as a fiercely independent teenager in small-town Kansas who believed women and men should receive equal treatment, I would have given the same answer. So much of what ails our country now, in matters of gender and many other issues, is that we are not speaking the same language.

In the context of her native class, Parton's gift to young women is not a statement but an example. One wishes for both from a hero. But, if I could only have one of the two, I'd pick the latter.

Parton's example is not lost on today's female creators. In 2011, a Canadian film set in rural Winnipeg in the 1970s told the story of a girl discovering she's adopted just as she's hitting puberty. She turns to her Dolly Parton records and gets it in her head that Parton is her mom. The film, *The Year Dolly Parton Was My Mom*, is self-aware in its feminist messages. Hoping to use Parton's music in the film, writer-director Tara Johns managed to get the script to her through a series of contacts just before Parton left on tour.

Parton responded with a faxed letter stating that she had spent the weekend reading the script and was over the moon, Johns told women's lifestyle website She Does the City. Parton gave her rights to use nine songs for a small fee, four of which were re-recorded by Canadian artists, including Nelly Furtado and the Wailin' Jennys.

"No Canadian film could afford to buy those publishing rights at the going rate," Johns said. Parton even recorded a voiceover for the film, which Johns had the idea for after hearing Parton in a radio interview.

"I'd never really listened to Dolly Parton. I mean, the music, yes, but not the woman. Because there were no distractions, no flashy sequins or hair or boobs or whatever, it was just really easy to listen to the substance, and I

was blown away by how strong a career woman she was, even way back when," Johns said. "She blazed a trail for so many artists who came after her, and I didn't know that about her. That was a bit of a revelation. I thought it would have been cool when I was 11 or 12 to know that Dolly Parton was a feminist, under all of that."

Johns noted that Parton's pioneering feminism might have been overlooked for the way she went about it. "The whole objectification that most woman rail against, she took it, and she went to the wall with it," Johns said. "And in a way, it's a challenge, she sort of challenged that whole concept, that whole way of looking at women. You scrape the very thin veneer of that objectified image and you get so much substance."

If in doubt that Parton's performance is always deeper than it seems, see her 2013 appearance on *The Queen Latifah Show*, soon after Latifah starred in the 2012 remake of *Steel Magnolias*, which featured an all-black female cast, with Jill Scott playing Parton's iconic beautician character Truvy. In an apparent homage to Latifah, with whom she costarred in the 2012 musical gospel film *Joyful Noise*, Parton performed an original rap in a blond afro wig. The song had an early hip-hop, Grandmaster Flash-style hook and a classic rap theme — don't try to step to this — while telling the story of her life.

"Please welcome one of the baddest rappers in the game, straight out of the 'ville," Latifah said to introduce the segment. "Nashville, that is."

Parton started with the classic hip-hop audience exchange — "Hey, hoooo, hey, hoooo" — and then broke into full East Tennessee: "I'm not callin' nobody names. I'm just sayin' how-*deeee*!"

Parton then pointed out that she and Latifah both have large breasts, but that only one of them is really known for working them. She gestured down at her chest in a skin-tight black leotard with, as ever, long sleeves (she is rumored to be covered in tattoos).

"Look at dem go!" she rapped about her breasts. "Hey, I'm tweakin. I'm workin'. I'm twerkin'. Hey, Miley — I got your wreckin' balls right *heeya*." Parton adds to that last word a breath that is a feature of Southern Protestant dialect. Soon she was singing, "She'll be comin' around the mountain when she comes," over the beat.

The performance is uncomfortable. In inviting Latifah to battle, she

referenced belonging to a "redneck mafia," apparently without realizing this might conjure for some viewers the violent and deadly horrors of white supremacy in the South. It seems that Parton's awkward intention was to tell Latifah's audience that she, too, was an "Other" of sorts, finding her way out of the role society assigned her by performing it.

"You may be the queen," Parton said, "but I am the white-trash princess. Well, me and Honey Boo Boo." Her joke reference to a hit reality show about a child beauty pageant contestant and her "trailer trash" family was poignant in that Parton understands the exploitation at work in such entertainment. Like the little girl, she has been the punchline of late-night talk show jokes. But Honey Boo Boo had no choice and, to some extent, the family that was offered a much-needed check from the TLC network didn't either.

Whether they live in trailer parks or elsewhere, perhaps little girls coming of age right now — when Parton is a shining crone in full command of her own character's contradictions — have a better chance of understanding the feminist significance of Parton's lifelong performance, lost on many of us until recent years. (Parton might be thinking so, too; her first-ever children's album was released this fall.)

And young female artists are picking up where Parton leaves off. Minaj twerks while she dares you to degrade her, calls out Parton protégé Miley Cyrus for cultural appropriation, and makes sure her curves are in your face while she does it. Indeed, she ends a rap appearance on the Drake song "Make Me Proud" with a direct invocation of the country singer's name: "Double D up, hoes. Dolly Parton."

God's Little Dolly Parton

Part of Parton's power as a woman is that she has preserved something of the child she once was, not just as the main character in a song about a coat sewn from rags but in her a sense of wonder about the world.

In one of the more startling passages of her autobiography, *Dolly: My Life and Other Unfinished Business* — mostly a mix of retold stories, country-isms, and carefully chosen "revelations" about the woman behind the career — Parton describes a primal, even pagan joy about the natural world.

Parton is now to country music what Oprah Winfrey is to media — a natural talent who, simply by being herself, transcended an industry to transform society.

"Sometimes I like to run naked in the moonlight and the wind, on the little trail behind our house, when the honeysuckle blooms," Parton wrote. "It's a feeling of freedom, so close to God and nature."

One might find this claim fantastical and dubious in other celebrity memoirs, but Parton has only described what she once knew as a child: the feral liberty of the poor child whose parents are hard at work while she entertains herself. Parton's rural upbringing, not to mention the star inside her that set her apart from other kids, meant that her closest friend was the Earth itself. It's easy to believe that an icon known for her groundedness has been recreating that experience on a trail through her Tennessee compound.

"The full moon is my best time," Parton wrote. "It's a good feeling to have no makeup, no wig, no high heels, just my little stubby self. Just God's little Dolly Parton again."

This is the spirituality — erotic, embodied, without need of man or church — that has been Parton's touchstone since her early days. In Dolly, she counted three loves that most shaped her: God, music, and sex. They are all plain to see in rural East Tennessee: the harsh Pentecostal faith of her pastor grandfather, the homemade instruments she played barefoot on porches, the 12 children her mother had for lack of birth control and need of farm help.

Parton, like her creative mother with a box of rags, has refashioned and sewn these themes together to create her own authentic life. While building a career on music, Parton claimed sexual power — not just in relationship to a partner but in relationship to the entire world — and carried herself with a faith that expresses itself through Christianity but finds its power within rather than without ("The magic is inside you," Parton has said. "There ain't no crystal ball.")

In her autobiography, Parton mused that she dreamed about creating a line of high-quality bras for large-chested women because she loved lingerie and found it lacking in her size. Her next thought is a loving kiss-off to the pastor grandfather who, when she was

a teenager, shamed her as a harlot for wearing makeup and tight clothes. "Grandpa Jake is in heaven now," she wrote. "I hope he's getting a kick out of seeing me go into business hawking the very things he used to chastise me for."

In constructing the story of her life and its representation through interviews, live performances, books, and autobiographical TV movies, Parton has masterfully recreated the female story and image that patriarchy tries to remove: that of the woman who is in possession of herself as a powerful force at once sexual and godlike.

In the seminal 1992 feminist text *Women Who Run with the Wolves: Myths and Stories of the Wild Woman Archetype*, Jungian psychoanalyst Clarissa Pinkola Estés exhumed an archetype she said had been deliberately removed from myths, religious stories, and culture altogether.

This is how many women's teaching tales about sex, love, money, marriage, birthing, death, and transformation were lost. It is how fairy tale and myths that explicate ancient women's mysteries have been covered over too. Most old collections of fairy tales and mythos existent today have been scoured clean of the scatological, the sexual, the perverse (as in warnings against), the pre-Christian, the feminine, the Goddesses, the initiatory, the medicines for various psychological malaises, and the directions for spiritual raptures.

The Wild Woman, as Estés writes, "can be redrawn accurately — often revealing amazing understructures which begin to heal women's sadness that so much of the old mysteries has been destroyed."

As a child, I was lucky to be surrounded by people from many of the old European countries and Mexico. ...]They, and many others — Native Americans, people from Appalachia, Asian immigrants, and many African-American families from the South — came to farm, to pick, to work in the ash

pits and steel mills, the breweries, and in domestic jobs. Most were not educated in the academic sense, yet they were intensely wise. They were the bearers of a valuable and almost pure oral tradition.

The removal of women from country radio by male executives is but an echo of the removal of feminine power from biblical stories by powerful men. Neither, we see from Parton's songwriting, life, and career, can stop a woman from being heard. She has picked up where female apostle Mary Magdalene — by some interpretations, a sexually free female who followed Christ — left off in the New Testament to become our modern-day patroness of the wayward woman, the Wild Woman of myth and feminist texts.

That woman was in full glory during the 1989 Country Music Awards. Parton performed the Don Francisco gospel song "He's Alive," which she covered on that year's *White Limozeen* album, after being moved by the song when she heard it one night on her tour bus. At the CMA performance, alone onstage, a tight white gown covered her from neck to wrist to ankle but clung to her curves. Her big blonde wig and shiny red lips were not the stuff of modesty.

The song tells the story of Jesus' resurrection through the eyes of Peter, who at first doesn't believe the first person to see Jesus alive after his tomb was found empty — Mary Magdalene.

We both ran toward the garden then John ran on ahead,
We found the stone and the empty tomb just the way that Mary said,
But the winding sheet they wrapped him in was just an empty shell,
And how or where they'd taken him was more than I could tell.

Parton sang it with trepidation in her voice and on her face, her head cocked and eyes a bit glazed, like she was channeling the song from somewhere else. Eventually, as goes the Bible story and the song, Peter sees the resurrected Jesus with his own eyes and is overwhelmed with a sense of peace, joy, and release. A bridge comes in, changing the key of the song, and Parton conveyed the epiphany by lifting her arms. As she did so, a stage-wide screen behind her was supposed to rise, apparently; there was some sort of technical glitch, it seemed, and Parton turned back to the microphone to begin the triumphant breakthrough verse with her clear, booming pipes: "He's alive!" As she did, the screen finally came up, revealing a large choir in angelic robes who, as in the recorded song, echoed "He's alive" higher on the scale.

I haven't belonged to the Christian faith in nearly 25 years, but watching the old performance online gave me goosebumps and nearly brought me to tears — not for the religion in it but for the transcendent accomplishment of the song, the voices, the woman at the front of the stage in utter command, possessed by her own performance.

The song so thoroughly destroyed the auditorium full of country music performers that, as the camera panned to the crowd, at least one older man could be seen weeping. There was a moment, then, when Parton seemed to realize what had just happened. Her eyes became clear and focused on the crowd, and her face took on a satisfied look that seemed to say, "Wow, we just brought this bitch down." Before thanking the choir, she swaggered backward with a swing in her hips. She had just accomplished her professional mission: to see God in a song, and in the process let the whole world see her.

Don't Need No Company

Early in Dolly Parton's career, when her lifelong best friend, Judy, got out of the Air Force, the two took a trip to New York to live it up with Parton's new money from *The Porter Wagoner Show*. She was a country TV star but could still go relatively unrecognized in New York City, according to *Dolly: My Life and Other Unfinished Business*. The pair put on tight skirts and heavy makeup and went out on the town — each with a .38-caliber handgun in her purse. "I felt comfortable enough around a gun, and at that time I thought carrying one was the thing to do," Parton wrote.

New York was a grittier place then, around 1970, and they were 20-something country girls from the same holler on a mission: to be bad. They found a seedy movie theater and settled in to watch a porn. This attempt at a bit of harmless scandal turned out to be uncomfortable,

though — two young women in a bad-smelling theater with a handful of men who were "the raincoat type." The movie itself disturbed them. "What we thought would be exciting and sexy was gross, filthy, and insulting," Parton wrote. She and Judy walked out.

A few blocks down the street, according to the book, they leaned against a wall — "dressed the way we were" — to collect themselves. A drunk man asked Parton for her rate as a prostitute. She told him to get lost. "We don't need no company," Parton remembered saying.

In response, he assaulted her — "grabbing at me in places I reserve for grabbers of my own choosing" — and telling her she wanted it. Parton pulled her Smith & Wesson out of her purse, and he left. "I could hear him calling me a bitch as he walked away," she wrote.

Half a century later, Parton is as big a star in New York City and around the world as in Nashville, and her entourage carries the guns. But what is unique to her classic rags-to-riches story has a lot to do with that moment when a man mistook her for a hooker at the precise moment she was fleeing the degradation of a seedy theater. In the decades since, she has become one of the most decorated, respected, philanthropic pop-culture icons in history while dressed like "backwoods Barbie." She has cracked innuendoes with deep cleavage between a wig and stilettos whether doing a late-night talk show or receiving a distinguished honor.

"Am I asking for it?" she has seemed to ask with every appearance. With Parton a safe distance from physical threat, the "it" is the sort of "slut-shaming" every woman experiences but that those who dare to enjoy their own sexuality know best.

Parton learned early what people would see when they looked at her — a hot piece of female white trash whose appearance and sexuality warranted more immediate attention than her life's work. As she often says onstage, her mother used to tell her, "I hope you get a blessing out of it," and that's what Parton made of the unfortunate assignment society initially handed her. She is thus a woman of paradoxes: Someone who acts "trashy" and has more class than most. Someone who dresses "like a hooker" and, after 50 years in show business, is known as a shrewd businesswoman and a family-oriented, self-proclaimed homebody. A giggly blonde who is smarter than her male employees. A little girl who "got out" by singing about the place

she left. A Christian who is, well, a true Christian. A woman of extraordinary depth who came into the world named after a toy doll — a term of endearment that also suggests a dehumanized object that exists for someone else's pleasure.

"If I got any charm at all, it's that I look totally phony, but I am totally real," Parton told *Cineaste* in 1990. "That's my magic." True, she is a rare sort of icon — at once a sex symbol like Marilyn Monroe, a creative genius like Loretta Lynn, and a philanthropic empire builder like Oprah Winfrey. Parton performs herself and, if she is a whore, she is also the john turning herself out.

"You spent good money on me," Parton told the crowd during one of her 2016 arena performances, as if to say that she remembered what it was to scrape together money for a night out. How could she forget? That was the theme of half the songs she sang.

The audience, as ever, appreciated her memories of lean times. They might not hear her on new-country radio, but they roared with delight when she asked whether she should perhaps run for president.

In lieu of a presidential bust, in 1987 her native Sevier County installed a life-size bronze statue of Parton outside its downtown courthouse. In this representation, she is a young woman with her hair pulled back sitting on a rock with an acoustic guitar, her jeans cuffed at the ankles to reveal bare feet. This Parton is closer to the one who runs in the woods than the one who plays arenas in rhinestone-covered jumpsuits.

"After my dad died, one of my brothers told me that Daddy used to put a big oil drum of soapy water and a broom in the back of his truck," Parton told Jimmy Kimmel on his talk show in 2016. "And late at night he'd go down to the statue and scrub all the pigeon poop off."

Whatever sort of icon she is, whatever she represents to her fans and the rest of society — a wax sculpture wearing sequined shoulder pads in a Los Angeles museum of celebrity likenesses, a barefoot bronze in East Tennessee, or a living national treasure who defies easy categories — Parton survived and even changed a man's world so brilliantly that one occasionally sees on T-shirts or online memes an unlikely reference to perhaps the most powerful, least political feminist in the world. It's a line that, Parton recalled on Kimmel, her own father had on a bumper sticker on his truck: "Dolly Parton for president." ■

Contributors

ALLISON MOORER is a music industry veteran who has been nominated for Academy, Grammy, Americana Music Association, and Academy of Country Music awards. Her writing has appeared in *Guernica, Performing Songwriter*, and elsewhere. She earned an MFA in nonfiction at the New School in New York City, where she lives with her son.

CAMERON MATTHEWS is a writer, editor, and musician based in New York City. He previously managed editorial operations for The Bluegrass Situation and was the web editor for nodepression.com.

COLIN HAY is a singer-songwriter and former frontman of Men at Work. Hay was born in Scotland and raised in Australia, where a documentary titled *Colin Hay: Waiting for My Real Life* debuted at the Melbourne Film Festival in 2015. Hay released his thirteenth solo album, *Fierce Mercy*, on Compass Records earlier this year.

COLIN SUTHERLAND is an illustrator and designer living in the mountains of North Carolina. He finds inspiration in century-old fiddle tunes, vintage print ephemera, and the bawl of his bluetick coonhound.

CORBIE HILL is a career freelance writer who can most reliably be found in the features section of Raleigh's *News & Observer*. His work has also appeared in *INDY Week, Bandcamp Daily*, middle-grade science magazine *Muse*, previous *No Depression* print journals, and a number of other papers and magazines. Corbie lives on three wooded acres in Pittsboro, North Carolina, with his wife and two daughters.

DAVID MCPHERSON is a music writer based in Ontario, Canada, whose work has appeared in *No Depression, Words + Music, Paste, American Songwriter*, and elsewhere. He's also the author of *The Legendary Horseshoe Tavern: A Complete History*, released this year by Dundurn Books.

DAVID OLNEY has released more than 20 albums over four decades. His music has been prominently featured in ABC-TV's *Nashville*, and his songs have been recorded by Emmylou Harris, Linda Ronstadt, Del McCoury, Tim O'Brien, and Steve Young, among many others.

DREW CHRISTIE is a Seattle-based animator and illustrator. His work has been featured by *The New York Times, Huffington Post, The Atlantic*, and others.

ERIN LYNDAL MARTIN received her MFA in poetry from the University of Alabama. Her work has appeared in *The Rumpus, Salon, The Quietus*, and elsewhere. Her favorite things are birthday cake and napping with the air conditioner on.

HENRY CARRIGAN writes a weekly column about music books for nodepression.com and is sales and marketing manager for *No Depression* in print. He also writes about music and books for *Living Blues, Downbeat, Publishers Weekly*, and *BookPage*.

JANIS IAN is a singer-songwriter now in her fifth decade of performing. She began her mostly stellar, sometimes stormy professional life at the age of 12 when she wrote her first song and was published by *Broadside* magazine. She received her most recent Grammy nomination in 2016, making a total of 10 nominations over the years in eight categories.

JENNY RITTER is one of those full-time musicians who still needs a creative hobby, so you'll find her acrylic and ink illustrations popping up all over the music world. This wearer of many hats leads a band under her own name and runs a couple of rock and roll choirs in Vancouver, British Columbia.

JESSICA HUSBAND, who grew up in Dallas, Pennsylvania, is a painter and illustrator. She specializes in telling life and love journeys through personalized commissioned illustrations. Jessie lives in Philadelphia with her partner and 3-year-old son, Gus.

JOHN KRUTH is the author of *To Live's To Fly: The Ballad of the Late, Great Townes Van Zandt* (2007, DaCapo Press) and *Rhapsody in Black: The Life & Music of Roy Orbison* (2013, BackBeat/Hal Leonard Books). His new book, *A Friend of the Devil: The Glorification of the Outlaw in Song from Robin Hood to Rap*, was released in September by BackBeat/Hal Leonard Books. Kruth's writing has appeared in *The New York Times, Rolling Stone, Sing Out!*, and elsewhere. He lives in New York City and Split, Croatia.

JONATHAN BERNSTEIN is a writer and fact-checker living in Brooklyn. His work has been published in the *Oxford American, The Guardian, Rolling Stone, Pitchfork*, and *American Songwriter*.

KELLY MCCARTNEY has logged nearly 30 years in the music business. She currently serves as the editorial director for The Bluegrass Situation and host/producer of Hangin' & Sangin'. She also contributes to *No Depression, Folk Alley*, and *Curve*.

KIM RUEHL is a recovering songwriter who unexpectedly landed in a job as a music writer in 2005. Since then, her work has been published in *Billboard, Yes, Seattle Weekly*, NPR, and elsewhere. She's the outgoing editor-in-chief of *No Depression* and is working on a book about the life and times of folk song collector and labor/civil rights activist Zilphia Horton. She lives in Asheville, North Carolina.

SARAH SMARSH is a journalist who writes about socioeconomic class in America. She has reported on public policy for *Harper's*, NewYorker.com, *The Guardian, Guernica*, and others. Her essays on cultural boundaries have been published by *Aeon, McSweeney's*, and more. She formerly reviewed female country acts for alt-weeklies in the Midwest. Smarsh's book on the working poor and her upbringing in rural Kansas is forthcoming from Scribner. She lives in Kansas and Texas.

STEPHEN DEUSNER is a Tennessee native now living in Bloomington, Indiana. His work appears regularly in *Pitchfork, American Songwriter, Uncut*, The Bluegrass Situation, *Stereogum, Salon*, and elsewhere.

Screen Door

IN PRAISE OF SILENCE

BY JANIS IAN

As songwriters, we're not about silence; we're about noise. We fill the empty air with music, stuff an empty page with song. So why praise silence?

Because it's our most powerful tool.

Most of us exist in a perpetual whirlwind of "now." Not in the Zen sense of connecting to the moment and the universe, but a frenetic dance of email, phone, car, work, car, dinner, then exercising in front of an iPad to lower our blood pressure before we implode.

That's not living.

Everywhere we go, there's noise, loud enough that a 2012 study by the National Institutes of Health estimated between 10 and 40 million American adults have hearing loss from exposure to loud noise. One in eight Americans over the age of 12 has hearing loss in both ears.

One in eight. If you're playing a festival with seven friends, one of you has significant hearing loss.

The noise is everywhere, often under the guise of "music." Mundane tasks that once bored us into creativity no longer exist. Instead of humming a song while we clean, we shove in earbuds that cover the vacuum's noise with music so loud it destroys the delicate cilia that protect our hearing. Instead of listening for birdsongs as we jog, we block out everything but the Spotify stream that keeps us moving. Go to a zoo and you hear cheerful Muzak coming out of hidden speakers. Go to a supermarket and yesterday's hits come at you from the poultry shelves. There is no "Sunday silence," where entire families could take a breather and regain their equilibrium.

In our era, we fear silence, yet without silence there can be no music. It's the silence that creates the rhythm, not the other way around. The rhythm is created by the space between the sounds.

For instance, we don't sing the notes. We sing the space between the notes. We manipulate the silence with sound. We use it to create space, and from there to create the magic and mystery that mark our craft.

Each bit of emptiness allows the listener a moment of unconscious reflection.

Of course, what I'm calling "silence" isn't actual silence, because the world itself is never silent. If you could throw yourself back to the beginning of humankind, your ears would be filled with the sound of wind rustling through prairie grass, animals roaring out their frustration across an empty plain. The sound of wood crackling in a fire pit, of fat spattering into the flames as dinner cooked. Now, we're cut off from that kind of natural "silence." We've replaced nature with noise, ocean waves with sleep therapy machines.

But silence slows us down, gives us breathing room, reminds us that we are part of a bigger world. Ask anyone with hearing aids, and they will agree that listening is exhausting. Listening demands attention, and our attention is so easily diverted these days, it's barely available.

As a performer, I've noticed the difference in audiences since we've chosen to fill in the silence. When I started my career in the '60s, an audience easily sat still for a one-hour set. As ownership of televisions increased — from being present in 0.4 percent of households in 1948 to 55.7 percent in 1954 and to 83.2 percent four years later — audience attention decreased. You could almost tie it to the spacing between TV commercials. At first, you had to break up every 30 minutes with a funny song, or a story. Then every 25, every 20, and finally, every 15. Nowadays, I suspect even that's optimistic. Two songs and the audience is ready for something new, a break to fill the empty space.

How do we counter that, in our songs, in our performances, in our lives? After all, we artists are also subject to the frenzied distraction of modern America. We're self-employed, tied to email because that's how everyone in our business does business. For me, countering the whirling means trying to leave more space — in my playing, and in my songs. When I solo, I try to feel the space rather than the notes,

because the more notes I cram into a bar, the less room there is for the listener to lean back and connect the threads I'm trying to weave. In my songs, I try to say more with fewer words. To leave more space in the lyric. To get more comfortable with silence.

I was recently privileged to attend a master class by the great buck dance champion Thomas Maupin (current holder of a National Endowment for the Arts' 2017 Heritage Fellowship.) You might think buck dancing and flatfooting have nothing to do with songwriting, but you would be wrong. Every master artist has something to teach us, and watching Maupin dance, I learned a lot about silence.

"Timing is putting notes in, and taking notes out," he told us. "When I'm dancing, I am the tune." He uses the rhythm of his taps to create a percussive instrument that becomes an integral part of the band.

He also said, "It's harder to dance too slow than to dance too fast." Just like it's harder to play slow than to play fast, harder to write fewer words than to write more, harder to sing like Aretha Franklin — putting in an occasional vocal run — than to over-sing and fill every possible gap with unnecessary notes.

Listen to any great song, and you will hear silence in use.

Moon river...
wider than a mile...
I'm crossing you in style someday...
You dream maker...
you heart breaker...

There's a pause after every thought, and it allows the listener to catch up.

When you watch a master artist at work, you're watching a tightrope walker. The audience holds its collective breath, waiting to find out what happens next. Will she stay or will she go? How does the chord resolve? Will that note hang until it decays completely, or will another note follow before I become so uncomfortable that I shut down?

It's easy for us, as songwriters, to forget that the first lyric we wrote was simple. The first chords we played were basic. We spent hours honing each song as we struggled to make sense of our talent and our work.

Remember that? I spent hours honing my words, writing out every bit of the song as I struggled with it, so I could see — and sing — the next part. There was a lot of silence going on, because I didn't know what I was doing yet.

I learned from silence then. It's time to start learning again.